THE
MOST
IMPORTANT
STORIES
OF THE
BIBLE

THE

MOST
IMPORTANT
STORIES
OF THE
BIBLE

UNDERSTANDING GOD'S WORD
THROUGH THE STORIES IT TELLS

CHRISTOPHER D. HUDSON
AND STAN CAMPBELL

BETHANYHOUSE
a division of Baker Publishing Group
Minneapolis, Minnesota

Published by Bethany House Publishers
11400 Hampshire Avenue South
Bloomington, Minnesota 55438
www.bethanyhouse.com

Bethany House Publishers is a division of
Baker Publishing Group, Grand Rapids, Michigan

Printed in the United States of America

Library of Congress Cataloging-in-Publication Data
Names: Hudson, Christopher D., author.
Title: The most important stories of the Bible : understanding God's word through the stories it tells / Christopher D. Hudson.
Description: Minneapolis : Bethany House, a division of Baker Publishing Group, 2019.
Identifiers: LCCN 2018053564| ISBN 9780764232862 (trade paper : alk. paper) | ISBN 9781493418664 (e-book)
Subjects: LCSH: Bible stories. | Bible—Theology.
Classification: LCC BS550.3 .H83 2019 | DDC 220.95/05—dc23
LC record available at https://lccn.loc.gov/2018053564

Cover design by Rob Williams, InsideOutCreativeArts

Christopher Hudson is represented by The Steve Laube Agency.

Produced with the assistance of Hudson Bible (www.HudsonBible.com)

19 20 21 22 23 24 25   7 6 5 4 3 2

To our colleagues at Hudson Bible.
We treasure every moment we can serve together
in creating resources that help people read,
engage, and apply the Bible.
Thanks for joining us on the journey.

Contents

Israel's Family Becomes a Nation

Kings and Prophets

Stories of Jesus

Stories of the Early Church

Introduction

The Most Important Stories of the Bible examines seventy-five stories throughout Scripture, from Genesis to Revelation. But (spoiler alert!) it won't take you long to discover that the Bible is really all one story. From beginning to end it details the flow of what God has planned, what God has already done, and what God has in store for those who love him.

These stories are presented in chronological order to help you understand the timeline and sequence of biblical events. Each one begins with a short synopsis that ties it to previous stories, and when appropriate, that synopsis shows how the significance of the story is relevant to stories that follow.

You might recognize classic "Sunday school" stories from the Old Testament, some parables Jesus told and miracles he performed from the New Testament, and other portions of Scripture. Search for new insights in those familiar accounts. Their impact, placed in context with those passages less well-known, should provide an eye-opening review of Scripture for longtime believers as well as a sturdy foundation for newcomers to biblical literature.

You might discover that some of your favorite stories are missing from this collection. Considering the scope and depth of Scripture, more content must be omitted from this book than can be included in the space available. In many cases you'll find only a sampling of one or two events from a historical era or a person's life (the judges, the prophets, the life of David, the life of Jesus, and so on), although so much more might have been covered. If you're looking for an account not included here, perhaps you'll review that story in its historical context as you're going through this guide.

Some people are quick to dismiss Bible stories as fiction or myth. They find it difficult to believe in giants defeated with slingshots, prophet-swallowing fish, or floodwaters that part to allow dry passage. The stories are presented here as they are in Scripture—as historic events, with no attempt to "prove" them. Rather than debating and defending our belief in the historical accuracy of the Bible, we've chosen to look instead for *why* each story is included in inspired Scripture. Whether or not you consider biblical accounts *factual*, you should be able to discern *truth* from them.

Becoming more familiar with Scripture is beneficial and satisfying (besides being able to answer challenging Bible questions on *Jeopardy!*), but Bible knowledge for its own sake isn't necessarily rewarding. As you read through these most important stories of the Bible, we hope they leave you hungry for more. The purpose of this book is to help readers go beyond mere Bible knowledge to develop or strengthen an ongoing, growing relationship with the Author of the Bible. Nothing is more essential than that.

BEGINNINGS

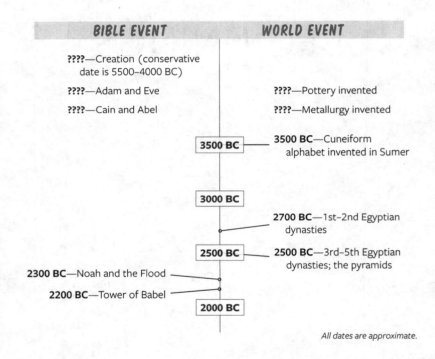

BIBLE EVENT	WORLD EVENT
????—Creation (conservative date is 5500–4000 BC)	
????—Adam and Eve	????—Pottery invented
????—Cain and Abel	????—Metallurgy invented
3500 BC	3500 BC—Cuneiform alphabet invented in Sumer
3000 BC	
	2700 BC—1st–2nd Egyptian dynasties
2500 BC	2500 BC—3rd–5th Egyptian dynasties; the pyramids
2300 BC—Noah and the Flood	
2200 BC—Tower of Babel	
2000 BC	

All dates are approximate.

Creation

The Story Begins

The book of Genesis opens with a clue that God is eternal: "In the beginning God . . ." Our world was just beginning, but the story of God has no origin. He was here before everything he created for us. He has always existed, and he always will.

The Essential Story

The earth wasn't a spectacular nor even distinctive planet. It was pitch black, barren, and just one of trillions and trillions of lifeless specks scattered across a boundary-less universe. But then . . .

The voice of God cracked the silent darkness, and light appeared. He coalesced the light, separated it from the darkness, and then called it a day.

In his next act of separation, on the second day, God spoke again. He divided up the waters, creating a heavenly atmosphere apart from the waters of the earth. Between them God placed a vault of sky.

Continuing the separation process on day three, God next collected the earth's waters together to allow dry ground to form. The planet was taking shape with land and seas. God deemed his creation "good," but the day was not yet over. God then established a variety of trees and seed-bearing plants, all with a self-sustaining capacity to reproduce.

Day four saw the creation of the sun, moon, and stars. In addition to providing light day and night, the predictable movements of the heavenly bodies were intended to establish the regularity of days and years and to "mark sacred times" (Genesis 1:14).

On the fifth day, the waters began to teem with all kinds of sea creatures as the skies filled with a colorful assortment of birds. The creatures of earth had God's blessing to "be fruitful and increase in number" (v. 22).

Land creatures soon followed on day six, both wild animals and livestock. And finally, in his ultimate act of creation, God made humankind. He also made some important distinctions at this point. To begin with, the humans—both male and female—were created in the image of God. They were also given the privilege and responsibility of overseeing the whole of God's creation. They were to both subdue and rule over the animal kingdom, and they had their choice of plants for food.

In addition, as God prepared to create humanity, he said, "Let us make mankind in our image, in our likeness" (v. 26). To whom was he speaking? Bible scholars tend to think either he was addressing the heavenly court of attending angels, or that the "us" was a reference to the collective Father, Son, and Holy Spirit that compose the one God of Christian faith. (Genesis 1:2 says the Spirit of God was hovering over the waters even before day one.)

God was finished with his work but not with his week. On the seventh day he rested. An omnipotent God never tires, so scholars again presume that his day of rest was a symbolic action, for our benefit more than for his. Indeed, the entire concept of Sabbath that became so vital to Jewish law and Christian practice was based on this example. As it was in the beginning, so it continues until this day.

Essential Truth

God created the earth, humanity, and all things, and he called them good.

Adam and Eve

The Story Continues . . .

The book of Genesis also provides a second creation account. The first was a description of creation on a grand scale. This one is more up close and personal, with much more attention devoted to God's relationship with his newly created humans.

The Essential Story

In the first five days of creation, God had spoken light and life into the blackness of the universe. He had separated light from darkness, atmosphere from waters on earth, land from seas. He had set the heavenly bodies in the skies. He had prepped the world for vegetation, watering the land with a mist rather than with rainfall. But before the land greened out, God determined to create someone to care for it.

Using dust from the ground, God formed a man and brought him to life by breathing into his nostrils. He placed the man in a newly planted garden called Eden, located in a lush and fertile area amid four rivers, including the Tigris and Euphrates. The man, Adam, was assigned to work the land and care for creation.

Scripture identifies two specific trees in the garden. One was the Tree of Life; the other was the Tree of Knowledge of Good and Evil—the only plant in Eden whose fruit was off-limits to Adam. (Little is said of either tree at this point, although both will be significant in the story that follows this one.)

In addition to his gardening duties, Adam was given the privilege of naming the animals. God paraded all the birds, beasts, and livestock before Adam, who gave them whatever name he wished. During the process (as God had planned, of course), Adam saw that all those animals had mates, that he was the only one-of-a-kind creature in the garden.

God had affirmed that everything he created was good, yet he knew Adam's lack of a human companion was "not good" (Genesis 2:18). God placed Adam in a deep sleep, during which he took one of Adam's ribs and created from it a woman who would come to be called Eve. We can only surmise that Adam must have been more than a little pleased when he woke up. Even though neither Adam nor Eve had human parents, they set a precedent that, from that point forward, "a man leaves his father and mother and is united to his wife, and they become one flesh" (v. 24).

The story pauses at this point with a telling observation: "Adam and his wife were both naked, and they felt no shame" (v. 25). It was an idyllic lifestyle in paradise that may sound too good to be true. We see in the next story why that degree of intimacy would not last long.

Essential Truth

As it's been from the beginning, God's desire is for humans to have fulfilling work, intimate relationships, and unfettered access to his presence.

The Fall

Genesis 3

The Story Continues . . .

Adam and Eve, newly created, were enjoying immense freedom in a lush paradise called Eden. They lived in innocence, experiencing no pain, no shame, and no fear as they interacted with God and the other creatures. They had access to a vast variety of food sources, and they had been encouraged to eat from every tree in the garden—except one (Genesis 2:16–17).

The Essential Story

One restriction. Just one. And not a big one at that.

Yet it was enough for one of the creatures to plant a seed of doubt in the humans' minds. The serpent, noted as more "crafty" than the other animals, sidled up to the woman and asked, "Did God really say, 'You must not eat from any tree in the garden'?" (Genesis 3:1).

It seemed like a simple yes-or-no question, but it was a cunning tactic. They both knew only one tree had been deemed off-limits, yet by misquoting God, the serpent craftily pulled Eve into a conversation when she attempted to clarify the truth. He made her suspect that God was hiding something from her. The more she thought about the fruit from the Tree of Knowledge of Good and Evil, the better it looked to her. But what ultimately sold her was the serpent's promise that the fruit would provide as yet unrealized wisdom. She took a bite and then passed it on to Adam, who did the same. That changed everything.

In an instant, the two went from being unashamed (Genesis 2:25) to hurriedly trying to cover their naked bodies with fig leaves. They had previously walked with God in the garden; now they hid from him. When God called them into account, the man blamed the woman, and the woman blamed the serpent, but their excuses were hollow. God passed judgment on all three: from now on the serpent would crawl on its belly and eat dust; the woman would become subject to her husband and experience pain in childbirth; and the man would forevermore struggle to make a living amid thorns, thistles, and sweat. And lest Adam and Eve then eat of the Tree of Life and live forever in separation from God, they were cast out of the garden. An angel wielding a flaming sword was positioned to prevent reentry.

Yet God's displeasure was tempered with mercy. Adam and Eve would die—eventually—but in the meantime God provided animal skins rather than leaves for covering (the first hint of death in Scripture). He also foretold an ongoing conflict between the woman and the serpent: in future generations one of the woman's descendants would suffer at the hands of the serpent yet would persevere over it (traditionally interpreted as Jesus' triumph over sin and Satan). The woman's offspring, Jesus, would one day undergo a much more intense temptation, but he would not succumb to it.

Essential Truth

Any form of disobedience to God is called sin, and sin separates people from God. Reconciliation is possible only because of his great love and mercy and through his provision of salvation.

Cain and Abel

Genesis 4

The Story Continues . . .

Adam and Eve, cast out of Eden, now have children. Their separation from God has led to their propensity to sin, which has carried on to this next generation. Sibling rivalry, it seems, dates to the very first siblings.

The Essential Story

Cain weighed his options and made a terrible decision. He told his younger brother Abel, "Let's go out to the field" (Genesis 4:8).

Cain steadfastly worked the soil to put food on the table, and he had endured dust, weeds, and sweat to bring an offering to God. But all Abel had to do was tend the livestock and then kill one of them. Cain couldn't understand why his offering had been rejected while Abel's found favor with God, and he didn't like it at all.

The Lord knew Cain's thoughts, of course, and he'd given him another opportunity: "If you do what is right, will you not be accepted?" (v. 7). But that opportunity had been accompanied with a warning: "If you do not do what is right, sin is crouching at your door; it desires to have you, but you must rule over it" (v. 7).

Perhaps Cain tried to come to terms with God's ruling, but he eventually decided he would settle the matter himself. He lured Abel into the field and killed him—clearly a premeditated action. As God had done after Adam and Eve's sin, he confronted Cain with a question: "Where is your brother Abel?" (v. 9).

Adam and Eve had made excuses, but Cain lied to God outright: "I don't know. . . . Am I my brother's keeper?" (v. 9).

God's stern response quickly let Cain know God was not fooled. Because the ground had absorbed Abel's blood, Cain was no longer allowed to work the earth. He had distanced himself from God, and now he was being separated from his livelihood, forced to become "a restless wanderer on the earth" (v. 12). The consequence of his sin struck fear in Cain as he realized he would become a vulnerable target of anyone who might want to kill him. Even though Cain had to leave his family behind and he "went out from the Lord's presence" (v. 16), God placed a protective mark on him. (Scholars can only speculate about the nature of the "mark" and an explanation for the other people Cain would encounter.)

Cain found a wife and started a family, but the little said about his successive generations reveals a rapid spread of sin, with references to evil, murder, and revenge. Meanwhile, Adam and Eve had another son, and they named him Seth. Seth's descendants, in contrast, would eventually lead to Noah.

Essential Truth

God cares more about our attitudes and motivations for our gifts than he cares about the gifts themselves (1 Samuel 15:22; 2 Corinthians 9:7; 1 John 3:12).

Noah and the Flood

Genesis 6–9

The Story Continues . . .

The problem of sin had never been worse. Adam and Eve suffered the consequences of their disobedience as had Cain for his crime. In a short time, the propensity to sin had proliferated until the whole of humanity no longer acknowledged their creator. It reached the point where "the Lord regretted that he had made human beings on the earth, and his heart was deeply troubled" (Genesis 6:6). Yet one person remained righteous.

The Essential Story

Noah thought the forty days of rain had been bad enough. He had seen the waters not only fall from the skies but also gush up from springs below to cover the earth. They had floated for five months before the ark finally settled atop Mount Ararat on dry ground. What Noah didn't know then was that his time in the ark wasn't even halfway over!

God's instructions had been precise, and Noah had followed them to the letter. The ark—450 feet by 75 feet, and three decks high—was big enough for what God had in mind, and Noah and his wife, along with his three sons and their wives, had prepared all the food and collected pairs of animals as God commanded.

More importantly, the ark had proven seaworthy. God himself had shut the door behind them, and the waters came. Then it was a matter of waiting . . . and waiting . . . and waiting.

After the Mount Ararat touchdown, it took another three months for other mountaintops to appear above the waterline. Noah waited yet another forty days and then sent out a raven that only circled the ark. When he sent out a dove, however, it was forced to return because there was no other place to perch. Noah sent the dove out again seven days later, and this time it returned with a sign of hope: a freshly plucked olive leaf. In still another seven days, when he sent out the dove a third time, it didn't return. Yet even then, after Noah removed the covering of the ark, the waiting still wasn't over. It took almost two more months for the earth to dry sufficiently to release the animals. When God finally said it was okay to come out, Noah and his crew had been in the ark a year and ten days.

The first thing Noah did upon his release was to build an altar to God and make a sacrifice. God reinstated human authority over animals, although from this point forward the creatures would develop a sense of "fear and dread" toward people (Genesis 9:2). Humans had evidently maintained a vegetarian diet so far, but God okayed a meat diet so long as the blood was drained prior to preparation. And finally, God told Noah and his sons to "be fruitful and increase in number; multiply on the earth and increase upon it" (v. 7).

God made a covenant with Noah, promising to never again destroy the earth or creatures because of human misbehavior (after earlier noting in his own heart that "every inclination of the human heart is evil from childhood" [Genesis 8:21]). God formalized the covenant by placing a rainbow in the sky—a reoccurring reminder of his ongoing mercy (vv. 13–16).

Essential Truth

Even in his judgment, God delivers the righteous and extends mercy to those who put their faith in him (2 Peter 2:4–9).

The Tower of Babel

Genesis 11:1–9

The Story Continues . . .

The great flood had been the result of unbridled sin on earth. God had promised Noah that he would never again destroy the earth in such a way (Genesis 9:14–16). Yet along with the reemergence of humanity came a renewed resistance to God.

The Essential Story

God's instructions to Noah and his family after the flood couldn't have been clearer: "Be fruitful and increase in number and fill the earth" (Genesis 9:1).

Subsequent generations had certainly increased in number, yet they had become blatantly defiant about the "filling the earth" clause.

At the time, all humanity spoke the same language. Determined to put down roots, they settled on a large and attractive plain called Shinar. Their plan was to establish a great city with a grand tower that reached to the heavens. By using bricks and tar rather than stone and mortar, they anticipated unprecedented success.

Building a city was nothing new or particularly problematic, yet the motives of the people reveal a severe underlying complication. They had two goals: to make a name for themselves and to keep from being scattered over the face of the earth. In other words, they were planning a life that not only rejected any need for God but also directly defied what he had clearly said to do— fill the earth.

We aren't told how far along they got with their monument to human pride, but the next thing we know, God "came down" to see the city and tower (Genesis 11:5). (If their goal was to reach to the heavens, they still had far to go!)

God quickly put an end to their delusion that they were all-sufficient without him. Rather than responding with a severe punitive action as he had done with the flood, though, he decided to "confuse their language" (v. 7). With the sudden inability to communicate effectively, the project was abandoned, and the different language groups scattered to various geographic locations, as was God's intention from the beginning.

The location of the tower came to be known as Babel, a name derived from the word that meant "to confuse" or "to mingle." In one sense, the name always harkens back to the language confusion of the Tower of Babel event. However, the name also became a synonym for "Babylon" in ancient Hebrew thought and writing. The mind-set of self-sufficiency and denial of any need for God aptly applied to Babylon as it grew into a more and more influential nation.

Essential Truth

God's will shall be accomplished, with or without human cooperation.

PATRIARCHS

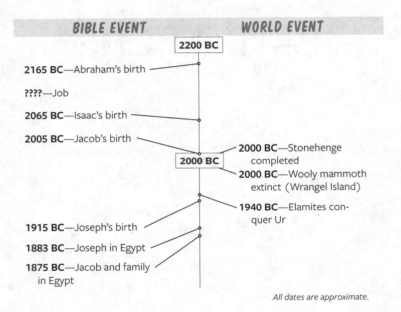

BIBLE EVENT | WORLD EVENT

2200 BC

2165 BC—Abraham's birth

????—Job

2065 BC—Isaac's birth

2005 BC—Jacob's birth

2000 BC

2000 BC—Stonehenge completed

2000 BC—Wooly mammoth extinct (Wrangel Island)

1940 BC—Elamites conquer Ur

1915 BC—Joseph's birth

1883 BC—Joseph in Egypt

1875 BC—Jacob and family in Egypt

All dates are approximate.

Promises to Abraham

The Story Continues . . .

Not too far from the plain of Shinar, where the Tower of Babel had been left unfinished, was a city called Ur. One of its citizens, named Abram, received a call from God to leave his home and head west to an undesignated location. Abram's obedience led to a name change, a late-in-life family, and the establishment of an entire nation.

The Essential Story

It was a big year for Abraham as he celebrated both his hundredth birthday and the birth of Isaac, his and Sarah's first child. (She was only ninety.) Twenty-five years earlier God had told Abraham he would become the father of a nation and only now was that promise starting to make sense.

Their names Abram and Sarai at the time, the couple had left a comfortable home solely because God told them to. They had no idea where they were going, but upon arrival in Canaan, God told Abram he would possess the land in every direction he could see, and then God established a covenant. It had been a solemn affair. God told Abram to try to count the stars as an estimate of the number of offspring he'd have. Then God told him his descendants would be enslaved and mistreated for four hundred years, yet God would bring them back to this land. The rite of circumcision was established at that point as a sign of the covenant. Later, their name changes were also signs of God's covenant, made when God promised them a child of their own (Genesis 17:4–8, 15–16). They both had laughed at the thought, yet God came through.

They'd made some missteps along the way, including some clashes with the land's inhabitants and a couple of close calls in Egypt, but God had protected them. Their current problem was a result of Abraham's haste to secure an heir. While childless, he had proposed passing along his legacy to a faithful servant named Eliezer, but God had assured him of an heir who would be his own child (Genesis 15:1–6). As time passed and Sarah got older, she offered her handmaid, Hagar, as a surrogate, and Abraham fathered a child with her. But the presence of Hagar and her son, Ishmael, had created repeated conflicts. After Isaac's birth, Hagar and Ishmael were asked to leave, but God promised to take care of Hagar's family. Abraham had never seen Sarah happier as she held Isaac, yet if he had waited for God to act, he might have avoided a lot of unnecessary tension.

With all the immediate household drama worked out and a child to raise, it appeared that life might be problem free for a while. Despite a few slips, Abraham had always been a paragon of faith. However, God would soon ask something of him that would challenge that faith—something unlike anything he had ever faced before.

Essential Truth

Real faith often requires obedience to God's instruction without our knowing the how and why.

Abraham and Lot

Genesis 13–14; 18–19

The Story Continues . . .

Interspersed with the account of Abraham and Sarah are a couple of noteworthy stories concerning Abraham and his nephew Lot. Although Abraham, remembered for his remarkable faith, is more familiar to most people, Lot is also noted as a righteous person (2 Peter 2:7–8)—a rarity in the culture where he lived.

The Essential Story

The herdsmen were arguing again. Abraham's nomadic lifestyle was becoming more challenging as larger and larger parcels of pasture were necessary to support both his and Lot's growing herds. Abraham had a simple solution: "Let's not have any quarreling between you and me. . . . Let's part company. If you go to the left, I'll go to the right; if you go to the right, I'll go to the left" (Genesis 13:8–9). Social etiquette should have prompted Lot to defer to his elder relative, but he was quick to choose the green and fertile Jordan valley, home of the cities Sodom and Gomorrah.

One of the early consequences of Lot's choice was that he found himself in trouble. Two coalitions of kings were at war, and the city of Sodom was invaded and looted. Lot was taken captive, along with all his possessions. One of his servants escaped and told Abraham, who immediately assembled a force of "318 trained men born in his household" (Genesis 14:14). They tracked down the abductors, formed a battle strategy, and safely retrieved Lot, his possessions, and many other people who had been taken.

But Lot's troubles weren't over. Sodom and Gomorrah had a well-deserved reputation for wickedness, and God alerted Abraham that he was about to destroy both cities. Abraham reasoned with God: Would he destroy Sodom if, say, it had fifty righteous people in it? God said no, he would spare the city if fifty could be found. Abraham kept negotiating. How about forty? Thirty? Twenty? Each time, God agreed to the number. Finally, it was settled that if ten righteous people could be found, God would spare the cities.

Yet the following scene from Sodom reveals its total depravity. God sent two angels to meet with Lot, although it's unclear whether Lot recognized their divine nature. As any gracious host would do, he invited them to spend the night in his home. When they said they would sleep in the town square, he insisted they stay with him. But before they even retired for the night, Lot's house was surrounded by "the men from every part of the city of Sodom—both young and old" (Genesis 19:4), all demanding to have sex with Lot's two male visitors. Lot did his best to dissuade the mob, even going so far as desperately offering his two virgin daughters as substitutes, but the townspeople would not hear of it. When they turned on Lot and were determined to break down his door, the angels took charge and struck the entire crowd with blindness.

The angels then told Lot they were there to destroy Sodom. They warned him to leave immediately and take anyone he cared about with him. Lot summoned his family. His daughters both had fiancés who refused to leave because they thought Lot was joking. Even Lot, his wife, and his two daughters were slow to respond, so the angels literally grabbed them and led them out of the city. The angels warned the four not to look back, but as burning sulfur fell on Sodom and Gomorrah, Lot's wife could not resist a departing glance. She turned into a pillar of salt on the spot.

From a distance Abraham saw the dense smoke rising from the area, most likely concerned about Lot's well-being. But as God spared Lot from what would have been certain destruction, God's thoughts were on Abraham's faithfulness.

Essential Truth

Everyone is responsible to God for their own actions, yet God hears our intercessory prayers on behalf of others.

Abraham Offers Isaac

Genesis 22:1–19

The Story Continues . . .

Abraham had rescued Lot from marauders and then interceded for him when Sodom and Gomorrah were about to be destroyed. Abraham had negotiated a truce in his own household after the birth of Isaac had created a rift between Sarah and Hagar. But Abraham had never dealt with a crisis nearly as challenging as what he would face next.

The Essential Story

What? Had God changed his mind? Abraham had heard the instructions clearly, but God had provided no explanation for what he wanted Abraham to do.

After waiting twenty-five years to have a child of their own, Abraham and Sarah had become a tight family unit with Isaac. That's why God's command made no sense: "Take your son, your only son, whom you love—Isaac—and go to the region of Moriah. Sacrifice him there as a burnt offering on a mountain I will show you" (Genesis 22:2).

After more than three decades of trusting God for direction and seeing that he could always be trusted to do what was best, Abraham decided to obey—and the sooner the better. He got up early the very next morning, took his son, and headed for the mountain God had designated. When they arrived three days later, Abraham told the servants who were with him, "Stay here with the donkey while I and the boy go over there. We will worship and then we will come back to you" (v. 5). Had he mustered enough faith to believe that somehow God was going to work this out? Or was he speaking out of desperation?

Any unsettled thoughts he might have had must have intensi-fied when, while climbing the mountain, Isaac asked him, "The fire and the wood are here . . . but where is the lamb for the burnt offering?" (v. 7). Abraham responded that God would provide the lamb.

Abraham arrived at the location, built an altar, stacked the wood on it, tied up his son, laid Isaac on top, and reached for the knife. Only then did God's angel step in to prevent the com-pletion of the sacrifice. Abraham had passed this one-of-a-kind test of faith. God supplied an alternative sacrifice: a ram whose horns were caught in a thicket. Because of Abraham's total obedi-ence, God also assured him that his offspring would be numerous and successful and that through them the entire world would be blessed.

In Hebrews 11:17–19, the New Testament explains that Abra-ham's faith was strong enough to believe that, if God needed to, he would have raised Isaac from the dead to fulfill his promise. In a sense, that's what happened. Isaac was as good as dead, but God delivered him.

Today's believers like to quote John 3:16: "God so loved the world that he gave his one and only Son." What must such sac-rifice feel like? Perhaps no one has ever come closer to knowing than Abraham.

Essential Truth

God never tempts us to do evil (James 1:13), yet he sometimes tests our faith. If we're certain of God's instructions, even if they are inexplicable, total obedience is always the best option.

Isaac Finds a Wife

Genesis 24

The Story Continues . . .

The blessings God promised to Abraham also benefited those close to the patriarch, including his family and servants. Lot had been spared at Sodom; Sarah had a child at ninety; and a substitute sacrifice for Isaac had been provided on Mount Moriah. Now, with Sarah recently dead and buried and Abraham growing older, Abraham wants to ensure that Isaac finds an appropriate wife. He entrusts the task to a dependable servant, but clearly it is God who leads the servant to the right woman for Isaac.

The Essential Story

It was a long way to go to secure one woman, but Abraham had made his servant swear to make the long journey to Mesopotamia because he wouldn't permit Isaac to take a wife from among the Canaanites. The 550-mile trip would take about three weeks each way and require ten camels for the provisions, gifts, and small group of companions accompanying the servant. In addition, the servant assigned this job had no definitive instructions for how to find just the right person. He needed a strategy.

He must have given the matter a lot of thought along the way. He arrived at his destination just as the local women were coming to a spring to gather water. As he saw them approaching, he told God he would ask one of them for a drink, which wasn't an unusual request coming from a desert traveler with ten camels kneeling nearby. But if the woman volunteered to water his camels as well, he would take that as a sign that she was the one he was supposed to choose for Isaac.

Before he had even finished his prayer, a beautiful woman came to the well and filled her jar. The servant asked her for a little water, and she gladly complied. He took a drink, and almost immediately she volunteered to draw water for his camels until they all had enough to drink. She poured the water from her jar into a nearby trough and went back for more.

Hers was no typical random act of kindness. She surely knew from experience that one thirsty camel can easily drink thirty to fifty gallons of water in a sitting. A gallon of water weighs eight and one-third pounds, so she had just volunteered to provide a complete stranger hundreds of gallons of water, weighing thousands of pounds.

After the camels had been watered, the servant brought out some impressive gifts: two gold bracelets and a matching nose ring. He asked to meet the girl's father and spend the night. She ran home immediately to set up the meeting, and she soon returned with her brother, Laban. Her name was Rebekah, and as it turned out she was a descendant of Abraham's brother. Laban offered gracious hospitality and care for the servant's camels, but the servant refused to eat until he had related his story. He wanted a response from them right away.

Rebekah's family attributed the chain of events to God. When they were willing to let her go to Abraham and Isaac, the servant bestowed additional gifts on Rebekah as well as on her mother and brother. The family asked for a ten-day period to say good-bye, but the servant was eager to return right away. They left the deciding vote to Rebekah, who was willing to leave immediately. The next morning Laban's family sent Rebekah off with a blessing, along with her nurse and other attendants.

When the entourage arrived back in Canaan, it so happened that Isaac was alone, meditating in a field. Rebekah prepared herself to meet him, and when Isaac saw her, he loved her immediately and they were soon married. Whatever peace and compatibility they enjoyed as a couple, however, would be challenged as soon as they became the parents of two very different twin boys.

Essential Truth

Many of the events we presume are coincidences may instead be clear—although unacknowledged—examples of God at work.

Jacob vs. Esau

Genesis 25:19–34; 27:1–46

The Story Continues . . .

Abraham had gone to great lengths to secure a righteous and worthwhile wife for Isaac, who had married Rebekah when he was forty. Even though Rebekah appeared unable to conceive, Isaac was walking proof that, with God, infertility wasn't always a permanent problem. Isaac prayed for his wife, and God responded.

The Essential Story

Rebekah wasn't just pregnant; she was resoundingly so. The activity within her womb seemed excessive, so she asked God what was going on. He told her she was not only with child; she was with *children*: "Two nations are in your womb, and two peoples from within you will be separated; one people will be stronger than the other, and the older will serve the younger" (Genesis 25:23).

The contention between the two began during their births. The first baby was born red and "his whole body was like a hairy garment" (v. 25). He was named Esau. The second baby, named Jacob, came out of the womb grasping Esau's heel. Jacob's pursuit of his older brother would continue for years to come.

Especially for twins, the two boys couldn't have been more different. Esau was an outdoorsman and a skillful hunter. He made his father proud. Jacob preferred home life, and he was Rebekah's favorite. Jacob also seemed to have a mental acuity and drive Esau lacked.

One day the twins were involved in their individual pursuits: Esau out hunting and Jacob at home, cooking stew. Esau returned, exhausted and famished, and asked Jacob for some of the stew. Rather than just giving him some, Jacob offered a deal: "First sell me your birthright" (v. 31).

In many ancient cultures, the oldest son had special status in the family. One of the primary benefits was that, when the family patriarch grew close to death, the son with the birthright received twice as much inheritance. Jacob caught Esau in a weak moment, and Esau agreed to the terms because he didn't have proper respect for his God-ordained family status (Hebrews 12:15–17).

The potential flaw in Jacob's deal was that the father had the prerogative to decide which son would receive the birthright-related blessing. One day Isaac announced he was ready to bless Esau, and Esau failed to mention that he had sold that privilege to Jacob. Isaac sent Esau out to kill some wild game and make his favorite meal, and Rebekah overheard their plans.

She came up with a plan of her own. Isaac was blind, so she would prepare his favorite meal using young goats from their herd, and Jacob would take it to him, posing as Esau. Jacob was naturally reluctant, because the brothers were so different physically. But Rebekah used the goatskins to create hairy coverings for Jacob's smooth hands and neck, and she dressed Jacob in Esau's clothes.

When Jacob took his father the meal, Isaac was suspicious. It seemed that Esau was back from hunting too soon, and the voice was more like Jacob's than Esau's. Isaac inquired directly: "Are you really my son Esau?" (Genesis 27:24). Jacob lied and said yes. Isaac asked "Esau" to come closer, but after he felt the hairiness and smelled the familiar clothing, he offered no more resistance. He offered a marvelous blessing, and even though it was acquired through deceit, it was legally irrevocable.

Jacob had hardly left the tent when Esau arrived with *his* meal for Isaac, and the two realized they had been duped. Esau wept and begged for a blessing of his own. Isaac did as he asked, but it was a prediction of difficulty, subservience, and a life of second best. Esau began planning to kill Jacob, just as soon as Isaac died, but Rebekah sensed the coming trouble and sent Jacob to spend time with her brother, Laban, back in Haran. Much good would come from that extended sojourn, during which Jacob would discover someone who matched his skill in deception.

Essential Truth

God occasionally uses people with questionable motives and actions to accomplish his will, perhaps because he sees who they will become rather than merely who they are now.

Jacob Becomes Israel

Genesis 28–33

The Story Continues . . .

Before Jacob and Esau were even born, God had told Rebekah that the older would serve the younger (Genesis 25:23). Yet Jacob seemed driven to manipulate events to control his own life. Stealing Esau's birthright, however, had forced him to flee to escape Esau's wrath. Jacob, the boy who loved to stay among the tents, would find himself working hard for what he wanted, heading a big family, and wrestling with forces larger than himself to become Israel, the man of God.

The Essential Story

Jacob found a smooth stone that would serve as a pillow and did his best to get comfortable for the night. He couldn't understand why Esau so loved life out in the open. For him, it was only a temporary necessity until he arrived at his uncle Laban's home.

Perhaps he drifted off thinking about how, even though he had gone to great lengths to deceive his blind father, Isaac had blessed him as he left home to start a new life. That night he had a remarkable dream of a stairway between earth and heaven, with angels going up and down. From the top, the voice of God promised him protection, possession of the land where he was sleeping, and an enormous family through which all other families on earth would be blessed. Jacob awoke, terrified at the realization that "surely the Lord is in this place" and "this is the gate of heaven" (Genesis 28:16–17). He made an altar of the stone on which he was sleeping and called the place Bethel ("house of God").

Upon arrival, one of the first people Jacob met was Rachel, Laban's daughter. He received a warm reception from the family, and then he arranged to work for Laban. Already in love with Rachel, Jacob offered to work seven years for the right to marry her. Laban quickly agreed. But when the seven years were up and the wedding night was over, Jacob discovered Laban had given him his *older* daughter, Leah.

Not accustomed to being deceived himself, Jacob confronted Laban, who cited the local custom of marrying off older daughters first. But, he added, if Jacob still wanted Rachel, he could work another seven years. Jacob agreed, but he never loved Leah as much as he loved Rachel.

One husband with two wives did not make for a happy home, especially when Rachel was unable to conceive while Leah had three successive sons. A frustrated Rachel offered her handmaid to Jacob as a surrogate, and the servant began to provide him children. Leah then offered *her* handmaid to Jacob. It got to the point where one wife was trading mandrakes (an herb perhaps thought to be an aphrodisiac) in exchange for sleeping-with-Jacob privileges. But in time, God finally enabled Rachel to have a son of her own, bringing Jacob's grand total (so far) to eleven sons and a daughter, by four different women.

When his fourteen years were up, Jacob was ready to go back home, but Laban realized what an asset he was; God blessed whatever Jacob did. Laban agreed to give Jacob all the spotted goats and black lambs he could find to start his own herd, but as soon as Jacob agreed, Laban gave all such animals to his own sons, and Jacob had to start from scratch. Deceived again! Yet Jacob used selective breeding techniques, and within six years he had larger and stronger flocks and herds. To his credit, he also realized by now that God was responsible for his success.

Laban, however, was becoming increasingly jealous and hard to work with, and Jacob knew it was time to leave. He tried to slip away, but a perturbed Laban caught up with him. They settled their differences and parted as friends, leaving Jacob with a new concern about how Esau would respond to his return.

One evening, shortly before arriving back in Canaan, Jacob lingered behind the rest of the group to be alone. A man showed up and started wrestling with him. The two struggled until daybreak, and Jacob refused to let go, even after the stranger forced Jacob's hip out of joint. Jacob insisted the other man bless him. The man said, "Your name will no longer be Jacob ["he cheats"], but Israel ["he struggles with God"], because you have struggled with God and with humans and have overcome" (Genesis 32:28). The name change was later formalized at Bethel along with God's assurance that Jacob and his descendants would receive the land promised to Abraham (Genesis 35:9–15). Jacob's sons would eventually become the twelve tribes of *Israel*.

Jacob took many precautions as he prepared to confront Esau again, but there was no need. After twenty years, Esau was glad to see him. Jacob settled in Canaan, although within another thirty years or so his whole family would be highly motivated to move south to Egypt.

Essential Truth

The quality of our lives tends to improve quickly when we stop trying to manipulate events and instead trust God to provide what's best for us.

Joseph: His Early Life

Genesis 37; 39–40

The Story Continues . . .

Of Jacob's twelve sons, number eleven—Joseph—would do the most to continue God's covenant with Abraham. In retrospect, it becomes clear that God used a series of unpleasant circumstances to eventually place Joseph in a position of power, but along the way life must have been quite confusing for a young man who was attempting to remain faithful.

The Essential Story

Doing time gives a man a lot of opportunity to reflect, so Joseph had to be asking himself why he couldn't seem to catch a break. His latest disappointment came after assuring a fellow inmate of the prisoner's imminent release. All Joseph had asked in return was for the guy to put in a good word about him to Pharaoh. But as each month passed, Joseph grew more certain that the freed prisoner had forgotten all about him.

Okay. Maybe *part* of this was his fault. Back home, he had been far too arrogant toward his ten older brothers. It was only natural, though. His father liked his mother, Rachel, more than any of the other sons' mothers, so it made sense that he would like Rachel's son best. Still, Joseph didn't have to make such a big deal about the multicolored robe their father had given him. Even better, Joseph could have kept his mouth shut about his two dreams where his other family members bowed down to him. But in his defense, he'd been only seventeen at the time.

He hadn't realized the depth of his brothers' jealousy and hatred until they turned on him in Dothan. When they found themselves with an unexpected opportunity, they decided to kill him. He heard their plan to slaughter a goat and spatter his beautiful coat with its blood to explain his death. Joseph understood why they didn't like him, but their cover-up story seemed a particularly cruel lie to tell their father. Thankfully, Ishmaelite traders had come through at that very moment, so his brothers sold him into slavery instead of killing him. Some consolation.

The traders carried Joseph to Egypt, where he was sold to a man named Potiphar, one of Pharaoh's captains. Soon Joseph was running Potiphar's entire household, with great success and considerable freedom. But Potiphar's wife wouldn't leave him alone; she kept trying to seduce him. One day the two of them were alone in the house, and she threw herself at him. He fled, but she managed to grab his cloak, and then she used it as evidence in a trumped-up charge of attempted rape.

Outraged, Potiphar immediately threw Joseph into prison. Before long, however, the warden delegated essentially all his work to Joseph. God gave Joseph success, and others couldn't help but notice. Joseph also demonstrated God's influence on his life by interpreting dreams. He correctly predicted one prisoner's death sentence and another's release. If only that latter prisoner would remember him.

The guy would remember, eventually. It would be two whole years later, but the timing would be just right.

Essential Truth

Despite repeated difficulties and no evident answers to our problems, we shouldn't be too quick to despair. God may use those very events to provide surprising blessings.

Joseph: His Egyptian Life

Genesis 41–50

The Story Continues . . .

Sold into slavery by his brothers. Falsely accused of a sex crime. Imprisoned and forgotten. Joseph's life between ages seventeen and thirty had brought one crushing disappointment after another. Many people would have given up along the way. Yet Joseph's faith in God seemed to grow stronger, resulting in one of the Old Testament's most impressive comeback stories.

The Essential Story

Pharaoh was troubled. Every time he had fallen asleep the night before, a weird dream wakened him. Seven thin and scrawny cows devoured seven other attractive and plump cows? Seven heads of grain, scorched and thin, had eaten up seven heads of full and healthy grain? What did these dreams mean?

Pharaoh summoned all his magicians and wise men, but they were just as perplexed as he was. Then Pharaoh's chief cupbearer had an "aha" moment. He might have smacked his palm on his forehead as he recalled serving time with Joseph, a prisoner who had a gift for interpreting dreams. Joseph was quickly summoned, with only enough time to shave and make himself presentable to Pharaoh. Joseph claimed no ability for interpreting dreams, but he assured Pharaoh that God would provide clarity. Both dreams meant the same thing, he explained. Seven good and abundant years were coming, to be followed by seven years of severe famine. The two versions of the same dream indicated that the event would happen soon.

Joseph advised Pharaoh to find a "discerning and wise man" to oversee storage of grain in preparation for the famine (Genesis 41:33). Pharaoh clearly had no one any wiser than Joseph, and so he promoted him on the spot to second-in-command over Egypt, complete with a signet ring, a chariot, an Egyptian wife, and other benefits. Before the famine arrived, Joseph had two sons: Manasseh and Ephraim.

The famine hit Israel as well as Egypt, but unlike Israel, Egypt had abundant stored food. So Jacob sent ten of his sons (Joseph's brothers) to Egypt to buy grain. As they bowed before the intimidating, powerful Egyptian governor, they had no idea he was the brother they had plotted to kill two decades earlier. Joseph knew them, though, and he remembered the dreams he'd had at seventeen.

Joseph didn't reveal his identity for a long while, nor did he make the situation easy for his brothers. He accused them of being spies and held one of them in custody until they returned with their youngest brother, Benjamin. (He was the only other son of Rachel, and Joseph was probably concerned for his safety.) Nine brothers were sent home with grain, and Joseph had arranged for their payment money to be secretly put back into their grain sacks, which terrified them when they discovered it. When they ran out of grain, they were forced to return to Egypt with Benjamin, against Jacob's wishes.

Joseph fed them all, but he gave Benjamin five times as much as the others. Then he released them all with a new supply of grain, this time having hidden his own silver cup in Benjamin's sack. Before they had gone far, he had them stopped. A steward opened Benjamin's sack to reveal the cup, and they were taken back to Joseph.

It seems Joseph was providing an ideal opportunity for them to turn on their youngest brother (again) for their own benefit, but this time they wouldn't hear of it. They pleaded that losing Benjamin would be too much for their father to bear, and one of them insisted on taking Benjamin's punishment.

Joseph was so moved that he started weeping loudly and uncontrollably, and he told his brothers who he was. When Pharaoh heard what had happened, he insisted that Joseph's entire family move to Egypt, because five years of famine remained. The family of Jacob (Israel) would remain in Egypt much longer than expected, but Joseph knew it wouldn't be forever. Before dying, he insisted that when God released the people of Israel, he wanted his bones to go with them (Genesis 50:25).

Essential Truth

As we become more aware of God's presence during unjust circumstances, reconciliation with others becomes far more satisfying than revenge.

Job

Job 1–2; 38–42

The Story Continues . . .

The book of Job is found in the "writings" section of most Bibles, along with Psalms, Proverbs, and similar books. It may have been written during that time, although the story appears to be set during the era of the biblical patriarchs, when prosperity was measured by the size of flocks and family and before the Mosaic law had been established. Even though the book provides few clues for establishing a historic time or location, the story itself is universal and timeless.

The Essential Story

Job led an enviable life. He had a wife and ten children who all seemed to enjoy one another's company. He was wealthy and renowned as "the greatest man among all the people of the East" (Job 1:3) in addition to being blameless and upright, one who feared God and turned away from evil. He regularly offered sacrifices on behalf of his children just in case one of them had committed a sin.

It was particularly inexplicable, then, when in one day he lost it all. Four messengers rode in, each on the heels of the previous one and each with a devastating report: Sabeans had attacked and taken all his oxen and donkeys, fire had fallen from heaven and destroyed all his sheep, Chaldeans had stolen all his camels, and in each case the attending servants were killed. But it was the final message that shattered his spirit: His children had been together when the house collapsed around them and killed them all. Remarkably, despite all these horrific reports, "Job did not sin by charging God with wrongdoing" (v. 22).

At least he had his health—but not for long. Terrible sores broke out on Job's entire body, from head to foot. He spent his days sitting in an ash heap, scraping the sores with pieces of broken pottery. His wife had seen enough. Her advice was short and not so sweet: "Curse God and die!" Yet Job was resolute and asked her, "Shall we accept good from God, and not trouble?" (Job 2:9–10).

Just because Job refused to complain to God didn't mean he understood his plight. In fact, most of the book of Job records a conversation between Job and his friends (three at first, and later a fourth) as Job desperately searches for logical reasons for his suffering. His friends offer every reason they can think of, arguing that he must have done something terribly wrong to deserve such a harsh consequence. Job refuses to concede that they might be right. He doesn't have the answer, yet he realizes they don't either.

Job's story is especially poignant because the readers are given information Job didn't know. We see that God was extremely pleased with Job's character and faithfulness. He had held up Job as a prime example of the best humanity can be, but Satan was convinced Job would be quick to curse God if his many blessings were removed. To prove Job's faith, God allowed Satan to test him. Job, however, never had any idea what was going on "behind the scenes."

After a lengthy and demoralizing dialogue among Job and his clueless friends, accompanied by an extended period of horrible suffering, God appears to Job out of a whirlwind. But rather than providing Job with sought-after answers, God confronts him with a barrage of *questions* concerning the forces and workings of nature (Job 38–41). The result is that Job quickly comes to see that the Lord is God, and he isn't. Halfway through God's interrogation, Job puts his hand over his mouth to signify submission (Job 40:4–5). By the end of God's questioning, Job repents and declares, "Surely I spoke of things I did not understand, things too wonderful for me to know" (Job 42:3).

After Job's ordeal, friends and family members flocked to see him, bringing gifts and consolation. God doubled Job's original fortune and blessed him with long life and ten more children, whose families he saw through four generations. After all his suffering, Job died "an old man and full of years" (v. 17).

Essential Truth

We won't—and can't—always understand God's plan and purposes. During such times, especially amid suffering and trials, we can have faith that God is still with us and will see us through them.

ISRAEL'S FAMILY BECOMES A NATION

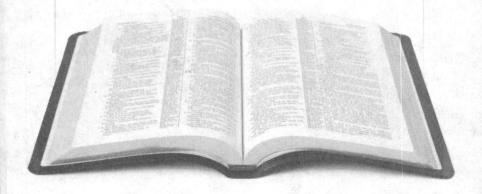

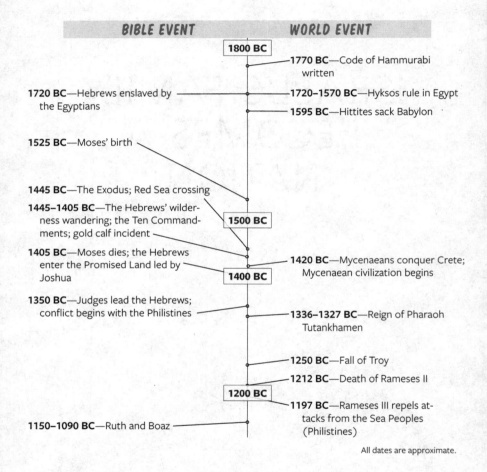

BIBLE EVENT	WORLD EVENT

1800 BC

1770 BC—Code of Hammurabi written

1720 BC—Hebrews enslaved by the Egyptians

1720–1570 BC—Hyksos rule in Egypt

1595 BC—Hittites sack Babylon

1525 BC—Moses' birth

1445 BC—The Exodus; Red Sea crossing

1445–1405 BC—The Hebrews' wilderness wandering; the Ten Commandments; gold calf incident

1500 BC

1405 BC—Moses dies; the Hebrews enter the Promised Land led by Joshua

1400 BC

1420 BC—Mycenaeans conquer Crete; Mycenaean civilization begins

1350 BC—Judges lead the Hebrews; conflict begins with the Philistines

1336–1327 BC—Reign of Pharaoh Tutankhamen

1250 BC—Fall of Troy

1212 BC—Death of Rameses II

1200 BC

1197 BC—Rameses III repels attacks from the Sea Peoples (Philistines)

1150–1090 BC—Ruth and Boaz

All dates are approximate.

Moses and the Burning Bush

Exodus 1:1–4:17

The Story Continues . . .

Jacob's family had moved to Egypt with Pharaoh's blessing to avoid a widespread famine, but that had been four hundred years ago. Pharaohs had come and gone, and the current one knew nothing of Joseph or what he had done to save the nation. All he knew was that the seventy or so Israelites had grown into a potentially threatening force of six hundred thousand men, and something had to be done about them.

The Essential Story

Moses rounded up the sheep and went looking for fresh pasture. He'd become good at shepherding over the past forty years—a life change that couldn't have been more different from his first forty years.

Back in Egypt, everyone had known him as the baby Pharaoh's daughter found crying in the reeds. Pharaoh had told Hebrew midwives to kill any male children born, but the midwives feared God more than Pharaoh. They spared the boys' lives, providing excuses when Pharaoh called them into account. Then Pharaoh ordered all newborn male children to be thrown into the Nile. Moses' parents complied—sort of. He was put into the Nile, but he was inside a waterproofed basket that floated to where Pharaoh's daughter was bathing. Moses' sister Miriam quickly volunteered to secure a nurse, arranging for their mother to serve in that role.

Moses had a unique education: raised among royalty as a member of Pharaoh's household, yet privy to the history and sufferings of the Hebrews from his mother (including the increasingly demanding servitude as Egypt tried yet another tactic to lower Hebrew birthrates). But Moses' two worlds collided one day when he saw an Egyptian beating a Hebrew worker. He thought no one would see, so he killed the Egyptian and hid the body. But the next day he discovered the word was out. Fearing what Pharaoh might do to him, Moses fled to the land of Midian.

That was forty years ago, and while life now was not as exciting as it had been, it wasn't bad. He had a wife, two sons, and a comfortable existence.

He noticed that during his reminiscing he had wandered to Mount Horeb, also known as Sinai. He saw a strange spectacle. A bush appeared to be on fire, yet it wasn't consumed by the flame. He went to check out the phenomenon.

When he got closer, God spoke to him from the bush, calling him by name. God told him to remove his sandals because he was on holy ground. Moses did as instructed. Then God explained he was aware of the Hebrews' sufferings and was going to do something about it. First he was going to send Moses to tell Pharaoh to let the people go.

Moses made every excuse he could think of, but God overruled each objection. He told Moses what to say, empowered him with impressive signs to get Pharaoh's attention, and agreed to allow Moses' brother Aaron to accompany him on this task.

God also promised to meet Moses back on that same mountain after the people of Israel were released from Egypt. But before that meeting took place, Moses was going to see things he couldn't possibly imagine.

Essential Truth

God doesn't ask people to do anything before first equipping them to do it.

The Plagues on Egypt

Exodus 5–14; 19

The Story Continues . . .

Threatened by the rapidly increasing numbers of Hebrews in their territory, the Egyptians have taken extreme means to address the problem, including infanticide and harsh imposed servitude. God has heard his people's cries and has designated Moses to persuade Pharaoh to let them go, but it will not be a quick or smooth departure.

The Essential Story

After hearing God speak at the burning bush, Moses fully complied with his instructions. He put aside his fears, approached Pharaoh, and demanded release of the Hebrews in the name of the Lord, the God of Israel. Now he was fast becoming the most hated man in two nations.

The Hebrews were first to resent him. Pharaoh had not only scoffed at the idea of their leaving but he then also increased their workload, maintaining their daily quota of brickmaking and requiring them to gather the straw they would need. The Egyptian taskmasters beat the Hebrew foremen when those quotas weren't met. The foremen complained to Moses, and Moses complained to God, who tried to console his bewildered servant: "Now you will see what I will do to Pharaoh" (Exodus 6:1).

Moses took his brother Aaron and went right back to Pharaoh to demonstrate God's power. Aaron threw down his staff, and it became a snake. The Egyptian magicians did the same thing using their "secret arts" (Genesis 7:11). Aaron's staff swallowed all the other staffs, but Pharaoh wasn't swayed. God sent Moses back the next day to impose a plague on Egypt. It was followed by another and another over an extended period.

As the series of plagues continued, Pharaoh and the Egyptians began to detest Moses as well. The waters of the Nile were turned to blood and the Egyptians had no water supply for a week. Frogs infested the land—including the people's beds, ovens, and mixing bowls. Gnats swarmed like dust across the nation, and then came swarms of flies. Egyptian livestock died. After five plagues, it had become evident to many Egyptian people that the Hebrew God was behind these events. At first, the magicians had been able to replicate the miraculous signs Moses produced, but after a plague of boils struck, they were so affected they couldn't even go out in public. In addition, the plagues were striking only the Egyptians, sparing the adjacent Hebrew territory. Pharaoh wavered a bit, and sometimes he would negotiate with Moses to remove a plague, but he never did so in good faith. He always reneged on his promise and refused to let the people leave.

The plagues continued. After the painful boils, terrible hailstorms arrived that devastated crops and injured the livestock and slaves of all who had ignored Moses' advance warning. A ruthless swarm of locusts destroyed everything the hail missed. And when it looked as if the situation couldn't get any worse, a thick darkness fell across Egypt, so severe that it prevented all activity for three days, although the people of Israel had light.

Moses forewarned Pharaoh of a final plague that would take the lives of every firstborn son, both human and animal. It would be so catastrophic that it would certainly ensure the release of the people of Israel. Pharaoh had to know by now that Moses wasn't bluffing, yet he was defiant to the end, stubbornly refusing to prevent such tragedy.

Meanwhile, the people of Israel were making departure plans. Lambs were readied for slaughter at twilight, and their blood was applied to the doorposts and lintels of homes—a mark of protection to ensure that God would "pass over" those houses in his judgment on Egypt. The lambs were then roasted and eaten with unleavened bread. As Egyptians throughout the land—even Pharaoh—discovered the deaths of their firstborn sons at midnight, a great cry arose. At that point, Pharaoh couldn't get rid of the Hebrews quickly enough. The Egyptians thrust their gold and silver jewelry as well as their clothing on the Israelites to hasten their departure.

After 430 years in Egypt, the people of Israel were finally heading home. Their exodus continues to be celebrated annually in the rite of Passover, more than three thousand years later. Yet the journey would take far longer than it should have.

Essential Truth

The influence of average men and women faithfully speaking for God may be much greater than they could ever anticipate.

Crossing the Red Sea

Exodus 13:17–15:21

The Story Continues . . .

After 430 years as residents and then slaves in a foreign country, the people of Israel had finally departed. God had overcome Pharaoh's stubborn resistance, and the ruler had given his okay, but he was having second thoughts about releasing six hundred thousand able-bodied men from captivity.

The Essential Story

God had told Moses that Pharaoh was going to change his mind and come after the newly released people of Israel. But when the people looked behind them and saw the whole Egyptian army and six hundred chariots bearing down on them, they immediately panicked. Moses received the brunt of their fear: "Was it because there were no graves in Egypt that you brought us to the desert to die?" (Exodus 14:11).

God had seen to his people's release and was showing them exactly where and when to go, leading them continually in a pillar of cloud by day and an illuminated pillar of fire at night. He was taking them on an itinerary that avoided threatening opponents because they were a long way from being ready to contend with other nations. Now they found themselves caught between a surging Egyptian army and the Red Sea.

Moses tried to reason with the people but to no avail. God's advice was to keep moving forward. He told Moses to stretch his hand over the Red Sea. As he did, God sent an east wind that drove back the sea, walled up the water on both sides, and opened a path for the people to cross. Meanwhile, the pillar of cloud moved behind the people, creating a barrier between the two groups and lighting up the night to enable the nervous Israelites to make their escape.

The next morning, as the Egyptians renewed their pursuit, God caused their chariot wheels to malfunction and threw the whole army into a panic. They realized that the Hebrew God was behind their predicament. They prepared to retreat but too late. With the people of Israel safely on the other side, Moses again stretched out his hand, and the waters returned to normal, drowning the entire Egyptian army.

The people of Israel rejoiced and sang to commemorate their deliverance. Their faith in God was bolstered, and Moses became an instant hero. Their newfound enthusiasm, however, would be short-lived.

Essential Truth

God's people are often too quick to forget that their creator has absolute control over his creation.

The Golden Calf

Exodus 32

The Story Continues . . .

The development of faith can often be a gradual process; sometimes it never happens. The people of Israel had just witnessed God's power displayed in the plagues on Egypt and their miraculous crossing of the Red Sea. Yet every little challenge became a new source of grumbling and despair for them. God tolerated their whining for a while, but when such a habit goes unchecked, it can lead to worse problems.

The Essential Story

Israel's high spirits after their spectacular crossing of the Red Sea hadn't lasted three days. The first time they arrived at a location with no drinkable water, they immediately grumbled to Moses. God turned the bitter water sweet and then led them to a campsite with twelve springs and seventy palm trees.

Then they got hungry and again took their frustration out on Moses and Aaron, even wishing themselves back in Egypt, where at least they had food. (This would become a running complaint.) God flew in a flock of quail to feed them that evening, and the next morning they found a mysterious "bread from heaven" all over the ground (Exodus 16:4). They called it *manna* (meaning "What is it?"), and it would become a daily provision for the rest of their time in the wilderness. At another waterless location, after their whining, God had Moses strike a rock with his staff and water came gushing out. And even when they were forced to do battle against some much better trained Amalekites, God gave them a great victory.

All this time, God was leading them to Mount Sinai—back to the mountain where he had called Moses in the first place (Exodus 3:12). When they arrived, the people were warned not to even touch the smoking, trembling mountain under penalty of death while Moses and some of the elders, who'd been summoned by God, went to the top. There God gave Moses the Ten Commandments and an entire body of other laws to bring order to their lives (Exodus 19–30). The people were to become a community of faith. God also provided precise instructions for building a portable house of worship—the tabernacle—as well as guidelines for priests and other essential information.

Understandably, it took a long while for God to instruct Moses on all these matters. But when Moses didn't come right back down the mountain, the people revealed how little they understood or even cared about God. They told Aaron, "Come, make us gods who will go before us. As for this fellow Moses who brought us up out of Egypt, we don't know what has happened to him" (Exodus 32:1). Aaron should have vigorously denied their request, but he didn't. Instead he collected their gold jewelry and fashioned a calf, a symbol of strength in many cultures at that time. He proclaimed a "festival to the Lord" for the next day (v. 5), so perhaps he envisioned the calf not as a god itself, but rather a visible mount/pedestal for their invisible God. But clearly the people made no such distinction; they worshiped the calf and offered sacrifices to it.

God knew what was going on, of course, and he suggested destroying the whole bunch and letting Moses start fresh with another group. Moses interceded for the people, and God relented. Yet when Moses arrived on the site and saw the depravity for himself, he first smashed to pieces the stone tablets engraved with the

Ten Commandments and then relayed God's order for "whoever is for the Lord" to assemble and put to death those who were "running wild" (vv. 25–26). The Levites immediately responded, killing about three thousand defiant Israelites that day. (The tribe was commended and ordained for service to God for carrying out that difficult assignment.) Moses also chastised Aaron publicly, and Aaron responded with the pathetic defense that he had simply thrown the gold into the fire and the calf popped out. Moses ground the calf into powder, scattered it on the water, and made the people drink it.

No matter how much God did for his people, or how many reminders and warnings Moses and other faithful leaders gave them, the Israelites would repeatedly drift into idolatry and worship of the various gods of the Canaanites, even as the consequences of their actions became more and more severe.

Essential Truth

When God's people refuse to respond to his love, grace, and mercy, he sometimes uses other methods to get their attention.

Twelve Spies Explore Canaan

Numbers 13–14

The Story Continues . . .

The consequences of the golden calf incident *should* have motivated the people to repent and change their attitudes, but they didn't. As they all moved from Sinai toward the Promised Land, two of Aaron's sons were put to death for taking their holy priestly duties too casually (Leviticus 10:1–3; 16:1–2). Even Aaron and

Miriam were chastised for badmouthing Moses (Numbers 12:1–16). What happened next, then, should not come as a complete surprise.

The Essential Story

At last! They were finally here! The people of Israel were camped at Kadesh Barnea, a point at the southern end of "the promised land," awaiting return of the spies.

Moses had recruited one leader from each tribe to explore the land surreptitiously. The twelve spies were to evaluate the geographic layout, the number and strength of the inhabitants, the fortification of the cities, the produce, and so forth. One of the spies was Moses' assistant, Joshua.

After forty days, the spies returned with many stories. Two of them carried a pole between them that contained a single cluster of grapes. Others brought figs and pomegranates, which must have looked especially tantalizing for people on a manna-every-day diet. And the spies agreed on much of their report: "We went into the land to which you sent us, and it does flow with milk and honey! Here is its fruit. But the people who live there are powerful, and the cities are fortified and very large. We even saw descendants of [giants] there" (Numbers 13:27–28).

That's where the agreement ended. Two of the spies, Joshua and Caleb, wanted to move forward right away and take possession of the land. The other ten, however, vehemently opposed that plan. They added to their original report: "We can't attack those people; they are stronger than we are. . . . The land we explored devours those living in it. All the people we saw there are of great size. . . . We seemed like grasshoppers in our own eyes, and we looked the same to them" (vv. 31–33).

Upon hearing this assessment, the people raised a loud cry and wouldn't stop complaining. By morning they had determined to elect another leader to take them back to Egypt. When Moses,

Joshua, and Caleb begged them to have more faith, they threatened to stone them.

God immediately made his presence known to the crowd, and he again offered to strike them all down and provide Moses a more faithful following. Moses once more interceded for the people, but God had had enough. He forgave the offense, but he refused to allow the Israelites to proceed, sentencing them to wander in the wilderness for another forty years—one year for each day the spies had been gone. During that time, the complaining generation would die off and be replaced, hopefully by a group more faithful and prepared to move into the land.

Stunned by the idea that they would have to endure forty more years of nomadic life, the people mourned, confessed their lack of faith, and attempted to enter the land after all. Moses told them they would not succeed because God was no longer with them, but they tried anyway and were severely defeated (Numbers 14:39–45). Still, it was the only peek most of them ever got of the land that God had wanted to give them.

Essential Truth

Some opportunities God gives us are time sensitive. If we miss an opportunity, it might not come around again soon—if ever.

Balaam and His Donkey

Numbers 22

The Story Continues . . .

As Israel wandered the wilderness for forty years, their lives were anything but dull. Internal strife came to a boiling point when a man named Korah led a rebellion against Moses. It was short-lived; an earthquake swallowed him and all his supporters (Numbers 16). External conflict also became more frequent because the Israelites couldn't avoid contact with other established powers. Israel typically asked permission to pass through others' territories, but when denied they were drawn into battles where they saw God give them victory. They were quickly building a reputation as a nation to be feared.

The Essential Story

Balaam had spoken to a lot of animals in his time, but they hadn't been in the habit of talking back.

As a pagan freelance prophet of sorts, Balaam was hired by people who wished to pronounce blessings or curses on others. He had been approached by a king named Balak, who was fearful of the people of Israel camping nearby. They had somehow managed to break free from the Egyptians and were winning battles everywhere they went. Balak's territory was next in line, and he was willing to spare no expense for any help Balaam could offer.

But Israel's God had appeared to Balaam, forbidding him to curse Israel, and Balaam initially declined Balak's proposal. In response, Balak sweetened the offer. Balaam consulted God again. Perhaps he might change his mind? When God gave permission for Balaam to go ahead, the ersatz prophet thought he might be able to collect his fee after all. He was only trying to make a living, but his donkey was refusing to cooperate.

At one narrow passage the donkey ran off the road and into a field. Balaam beat her and got her going again. Then, along a walled path, she stopped suddenly, crushing his foot against the wall. He struck her again. Now, in the narrowest passage yet, the beast had nowhere to go and had simply laid down. A third beating did not help. Nor did his threat to kill her if he'd had a sword in his hand.

Then the donkey spoke: "Am I not your own donkey, which you have always ridden, to this day? Have I been in the habit of doing this to you?" (Numbers 22:30).

The donkey made good sense. At that point God "opened Balaam's eyes" (v. 31) and enabled him to see what the donkey had been seeing: an angel standing in the road with a drawn sword. The angel chided Balaam for beating his animal, explaining that the donkey had literally saved his life those three times. Balaam was still hoping to cash in on an opportunity that God had already forbidden, and God was not happy about it.

Balaam ended up blessing Israel instead of cursing them (Numbers 23–24), but he was not a changed man. On a first reading, he seems like a nice enough guy trying to obey God, but he was soon responsible for pulling Israel into sexual/spiritual sin with the Moabites (Numbers 25:1–9) and was put to death for his involvement (Numbers 31:8, 16). The New Testament states clearly that Balaam "loved the wages of wickedness" (2 Peter 2:15–16). He should have let his donkey have the final word.

Essential Truth

God responds not only to our actions but also to our inner thoughts, desires, and motives.

Joshua and the Battle of Jericho

Joshua 6

The Story Continues . . .

After a forty-year detour, the Israelites were finally standing in the Promised Land (Numbers 13–14). Moses had recently died, leaving

Joshua as a leader with a somewhat more faithful generation of followers. The people were finally beginning to obey and trust God, yet they now faced an intimidating task: take possession of the land, beginning with the great walled city of Jericho.

The Essential Story

Aside from the continual sound of trumpets, all was quiet. Conversation was prohibited, much less interaction with the perplexed inhabitants of Jericho peering down from the towers and windows of the city's imposing walls. Joshua knew from his spies' report that the people of Jericho were terrified of the Israelites. Word had spread about how the Israelites had crossed the Red Sea on dry land and their recent conquests of powerful kings across the Jordan. Yet this "assault" plan of God's was mystifying to both sides.

Joshua was following God's precise instructions. Each day the people assembled with a group of armed men in front, followed by seven priests blowing ram's-horn trumpets, other priests carrying the ark of the covenant, and a rear guard. For six straight days they had lined up, marched around the city, and returned to camp. Nothing of note had happened.

Now, on the seventh day, they were to march around the city seven times. Upon completion, the priests would give a trumpet signal, and the people were to respond with a loud shout. Then the walls would collapse . . . supposedly.

Joshua knew God had never misled the people. As Moses' assistant, he had witnessed God's power and glory displayed in mighty and miraculous ways. And after Moses died, Joshua had ushered the Israelites through the flooded Jordan River on dry ground, just as he had seen Moses do at the Red Sea. God was clearly still at work.

The priests completed their seventh lap. The trumpets sounded. The people shouted. (If Joshua held his breath for a moment, we aren't told.) And the walls fell, just as God had promised.

The immediate and impressive conquest at Jericho opened passage to the Promised Land—only the first of a series of victories for Joshua.

Essential Truth

Total obedience to God's instructions always yields the best results, even when they seem to defy logic or cultural norms. For those who respond in faith to God's commands, not even the most imposing problems are too overwhelming or insurmountable.

Gideon

Judges 6–8

The Story Continues . . .

Israel's exodus from Egypt had *finally* culminated with Joshua's numerous conquests of key Canaanite cities. Now each tribe was expected to go to its assigned territory and drive out the rest of the inhabitants. Otherwise, Joshua had warned, the Canaanites would draw the Israelites into idolatry and defeat (Joshua 24:14–28). Despite his clear warning, that's exactly what had happened (Judges 1–3). Enemies would arise and conquer Israel, the people would cry out to God, and he would send a warrior/judge to deliver them, but soon they would revert to idolatry and the cycle would begin again.

The Essential Story

This time it was the Midianites. An especially cruel and vicious people, they had ruled over the Israelites for seven years. They sat back and let the Israelites plant and grow their crops, and then they swarmed in like locusts at harvest time and took it all.

One day an Israelite named Gideon was hiding out in a winepress, trying to thresh a little wheat without being spotted, when an angel appeared with a strange greeting: "The Lord is with you, mighty warrior" (Judges 6:12). Gideon was anything but a mighty warrior, and he explained to the angel that his family was the weakest in his tribe and that he was the least in his family. In addition, everyone was currently feeling abandoned by God. The angel explained that God was sending Gideon to "go in the strength [he had] and save Israel out of Midian's hand" (v. 14). First, however, he had a simpler assignment: tear down the local shrine to Canaanite gods Baal and Asherah.

Gideon did as he was instructed, but he destroyed the idols at night, fearful of what his fellow townspeople would do. It was a good instinct, because when his actions were discovered, his peers wanted to kill him. He was saved by his father, however, who argued that if Baal were any kind of god, he ought to be able to mete out his own punishment.

However, before Gideon was prepared to take on the Midianites, he asked God for a sign. He left a fleece on his threshing floor overnight, asking him to make the fleece wet with morning dew while the surrounding ground was dry. The next day the ground was dry, but Gideon squeezed out a bowlful of water from the fleece. Still, he wanted one more assurance, asking God to reverse the previous test. The following morning the ground was covered with dew while the fleece was dry.

Gideon needed such assurance because God's "battle strategy" required much faith. First, God reduced Gideon's army of thirty-two thousand men to ten thousand simply by allowing the frightened soldiers to go home, but then he whittled the ten thousand to three hundred. And that wasn't all. Those three hundred were armed not with swords and shields but with trumpets, jars, and torches.

Gideon's army divided into three groups that stealthily approached the Midianite camp from different directions during the night. With a trumpet and a lit torch hidden inside a jar, they positioned themselves and awaited the signal. Then together, they smashed the jars, blew their trumpets, and shouted, "A sword for the Lord and for Gideon!" (Judges 7:20). Then all they had to do was hold their position as the panicked Midianite soldiers turned on one another. After that, it was no problem to call on other Israelites to join the three hundred in pursuit of their fleeing enemies.

After a memorable victory that required such faith from Gideon, it was disappointing that, late in life, he fashioned an idol and led Israel astray with it. Even so, the nation had peace for forty years.

Essential Truth

God doesn't choose leaders based on their status; he chooses them based on their willingness to obey. Still, cold and perfunctory obedience is no substitute for a genuine and growing relationship with God.

Samson

Judges 13–16

The Story Continues . . .

Like Gideon, Samson was a judge, although it would be hard to find two men more different. Gideon was tentative and self-effacing, but Samson was brash and defiant. Although his parents were conscientious and did all they could to prepare for their special child, Samson showed no signs of humility or dependence on anyone other than himself. But because God intended to intensify the conflict between Israel and the Philistines, he could hardly have chosen a better catalyst.

The Essential Story

Samson had his strengths, but patience was not among them. He effortlessly killed an attacking lion with his bare hands, and he created a clever riddle based around the event. Yet even though the Philistines had threatened to kill his fiancée's family in their desperation to acquire the answer to the riddle, Samson became outraged primarily because he had lost a bet. After he cooled off, only to discover that his bride had been given to another, he burned down the standing grain, vineyards, and olive groves that belonged to his offenders.

The Philistines, wisely not wanting to confront Samson directly, told the Israelites to turn him over. His own people put together a delegation of three thousand men to go ask him to give himself up. On their promise not to kill him themselves, he allowed them to tie him up and take him. As soon as they did, however, he broke through the new ropes, picked up the jawbone of a donkey, and killed a thousand Philistines on the spot.

Next the Philistines plotted to kill Samson when they discovered he was in one of their cities with a prostitute. They thought they had him trapped, but he pulled up the city gate, posts and all, and walked off with it on his shoulders. The next time he found himself attracted to a Philistine woman, though, they were ready.

Her name was Delilah. Each of the Philistine leaders promised her 1,100 pieces of silver if she discovered the source of Samson's strength. She would ask what it was, and he would make up something. Then she would do as he had told her, but his strength never waned. The men hidden nearby never got to jump out and capture Samson. After three such failed attempts, Delilah pushed even harder: "With such nagging she prodded him day after day until he was sick to death of it" (Judges 16:16).

He finally told her the truth: His hair had never been cut, and if his head were ever shaved, he would lose his great strength. When Samson fell asleep, Delilah again summoned the Philistine rulers, who came with the money they had promised her. One of them cut his hair, and then she woke him up. Within minutes Samson had been blinded and imprisoned, and he was put to work grinding grain.

The Philistines' mistake was in parading Samson around their temple to bring glory to their god, Dagon. Thousands of people came to witness his public humiliation. Placed against the supporting pillars of the temple, he prayed for strength enough to avenge himself. His final request was "Let me die with the Philistines!" (v. 30). He pushed as hard as he could, and the resulting collapse of the temple killed not only him, but more Philistines than he had killed during his lifetime.

Essential Truth

God uses all kinds of people to accomplish his will. What they get out of it, however, is largely up to them.

Ruth and Boaz

Ruth 1–4

The Story Continues . . .

The book of Judges describes a series of leaders of varying and often questionable character, whom God used to deliver his people in times of crisis. The book of Ruth, set in the same era, centers around two women with no influence or power, yet with outstanding character. God would work through them to bring a more lasting solution to Israel's lack of competent leadership.

The Essential Story

Now what? Her plans seemed to be changing every few months or so. Naomi and her family had moved from Bethlehem to Moab to escape a famine. Still, God was good. Her two sons had found wives, and the six of them had come together as a family. But then Naomi's husband had died. His death had been a blow, of course, but her sons would provide well for her. Then her sons both died, leaving the three women to fend for themselves.

At least the latest news from Israel was good: The famine was over, so Naomi knew what she had to do. She told her daughters-in-law, Ruth and Orpah, she was going back to her homeland. They began the journey with her, but then she thanked them for their great kindness and encouraged them to return home and find new husbands. Both were reluctant to see her go without them, but Orpah finally agreed.

Ruth, however, was insistent on staying with Naomi: "Where you go I will go, and where you stay I will stay. Your people will be my people and your God my God" (Ruth 1:16). Then the two journeyed to Bethlehem. Now what?

Ruth took the initiative. It was the season of the barley harvest, so she went to glean in the fields with other poor people and travelers (an allowance explained in Leviticus 19:9–10). It seems that word about her had spread quickly—especially concerning the care she had shown for Naomi. When the harvesting supervisor, Boaz, discovered the new woman in his fields was Ruth, he welcomed her and urged her to stay among the other women who worked for him. He ensured her safety among the working men, fed her well, and invited her to take water from their supply anytime. Unbeknownst to her, he also told his workers to leave behind plenty of grain for her to pick up. Ruth had feared her status as a foreigner might be a problem, so she was most grateful to Boaz. When she returned home and told her mother-in-law what had happened, Naomi was excited. Boaz happened to be a close relative.

Ruth kept gleaning among Boaz's fields throughout the barley and wheat harvests. In time, Naomi encouraged Ruth to make a bold move—to let Boaz know she was interested in marriage. Ruth took a bath, put on perfume and her best clothes, and waited until evening. After Boaz had gone to sleep on the threshing floor, Ruth went in and lay down at his feet. He awoke in the middle of the night to discover a pleasant surprise. Ruth explained she was asking him, as the family's guardian-redeemer, to take responsibility for her. He was more than willing, although legally he wasn't first in line and needed to work out the specifics with a closer relative.

Ruth stayed until early morning, but she left before anyone knew she had been there. Boaz sent her away with all the grain she could carry, most likely as a sign to Naomi of his interest in Ruth. (Modern readers may presume that the two took advantage of the privacy to start their romance, but the repeated emphasis on both of their characters strongly suggests that nothing untoward went on.)

Boaz cleverly acquired the legal right to redeem Naomi's property and inheritance—including Ruth. The two were soon married, and when they had a child, no one was happier than Naomi. They named the boy Obed, who later had a child named Jesse, who later had a child named David. Ruth the Moabite was instrumental in the family tree of David, the greatest king in the history of Israel. Later, through David's line, an even greater king would come (Luke 2:4–7).

Essential Truth

God brings joy to the lives of ordinary people, and he may have something even more special in mind for their future generations.

KINGS AND PROPHETS

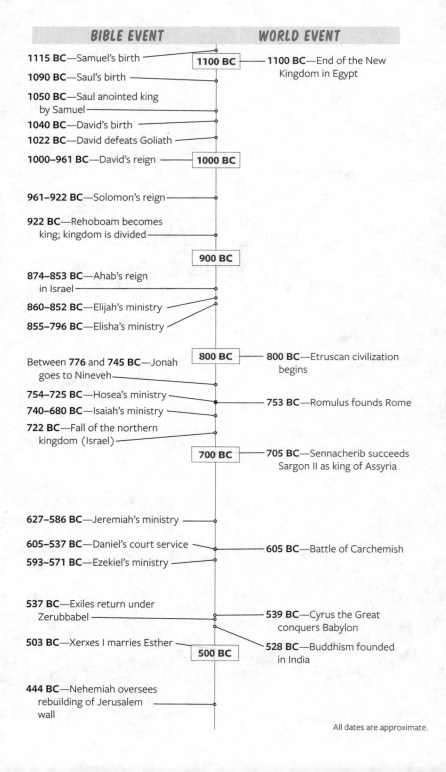

BIBLE EVENT	WORLD EVENT

1115 BC—Samuel's birth

1100 BC

1100 BC—End of the New Kingdom in Egypt

1090 BC—Saul's birth

1050 BC—Saul anointed king by Samuel

1040 BC—David's birth

1022 BC—David defeats Goliath

1000–961 BC—David's reign

1000 BC

961–922 BC—Solomon's reign

922 BC—Rehoboam becomes king; kingdom is divided

900 BC

874–853 BC—Ahab's reign in Israel

860–852 BC—Elijah's ministry

855–796 BC—Elisha's ministry

800 BC

800 BC—Etruscan civilization begins

Between **776** and **745 BC**—Jonah goes to Nineveh

754–725 BC—Hosea's ministry

753 BC—Romulus founds Rome

740–680 BC—Isaiah's ministry

722 BC—Fall of the northern kingdom (Israel)

700 BC

705 BC—Sennacherib succeeds Sargon II as king of Assyria

627–586 BC—Jeremiah's ministry

605–537 BC—Daniel's court service

605 BC—Battle of Carchemish

593–571 BC—Ezekiel's ministry

537 BC—Exiles return under Zerubbabel

539 BC—Cyrus the Great conquers Babylon

503 BC—Xerxes I marries Esther

528 BC—Buddhism founded in India

500 BC

444 BC—Nehemiah oversees rebuilding of Jerusalem wall

All dates are approximate.

The Call of Samuel

1 Samuel 1–3

The Story Continues . . .

The era of the judges had a few high points when God sent leaders to deliver the nation at crucial times. But overall, it was a sad and depressing period for Israel as they forsook God, and as again and again he allowed them to go into subjection to their enemies. It was time for a new kind of leader, one who would be consistently faithful.

The Essential Story

Young Samuel admired the new robe his mother had just dropped off. New robes were an annual gift. He likely wished he could see her more than once a year, but he did enjoy hearing her retell the story—how she had been unable to have children for many years, and how she had finally prayed fervently to God only to be thought drunk by Eli the priest. But then Eli had blessed her, and she had subsequently conceived. She had promised that if God gave her a child, she would give him back to him, so as soon as Samuel was weaned, he'd been taken to the tabernacle to be brought up by Eli.

It wasn't a bad life; Eli was a decent enough man. His sons, though, were miscreants. They were supposed to be priests, but they would take the best portions of people's sacrifices for themselves, and they slept with women on the tabernacle grounds. Eli chastised them, but they refused to listen. As a result, a messenger from God had told Eli that God would ignore their behavior no longer. Eli's two sons would soon die and be replaced by a *faithful* priest.

One evening, after young Samuel had turned in for the night, he heard a voice calling him by name. The old priest was losing his eyesight, so Samuel ran in to see what he wanted. But Eli hadn't called him, and he told Samuel to go back to bed. But twice more he heard the voice and went running to Eli. At last Eli realized it must be a divine calling, even though "in those days the word of the Lord was rare" (1 Samuel 3:1). Eli told Samuel that the next time he heard the voice he should respond, "Speak, Lord, for your servant is listening" (v. 9). He did, and God told Samuel what was in store for Eli's family—much the same account that the messenger had already delivered to Eli.

The next morning Eli was eager to discover what the Lord had said to Samuel. The young man courageously gave his mentor the bad news, and Eli accepted it as God's word. From that point forward, Samuel's reputation as a prophet began to grow throughout Israel. Eli and both his sons died soon afterward, and Samuel led the nation faithfully. He fended off the powerful Philistines, and he set out to rid Israel of foreign gods and pagan rituals.

But as with Eli, Samuel's faith and positive qualities weren't passed along to his own sons. He had hoped to make them judges, but they took bribes and otherwise perverted justice, so the people wouldn't hear of it. They wanted a king. Samuel realized that God was their king and that they were missing the point. He warned them that a human king would impose taxes and draft young people into his army, and he'd conscript more for agricultural, household, and other duties. No matter. They insisted, "We want a king over us. Then we will be like all the other nations, with a king to lead us and to go out before us and fight our battles" (1 Samuel 8:19–20).

God told Samuel to give them what they asked for. The Israelites weren't supposed to be "like all the other nations," but sometimes people must learn the hard way.

Essential Truth

One righteous person makes a world of difference in a culture deaf to God.

Saul: Israel's First King

1 Samuel 9–15; 28; 31

The Story Continues . . .

In their stubborn determination to have a king, the people of Israel had rejected both God and Samuel. Yet God provided a remarkable specimen of a man to be their first king. Saul was noticeably taller than anyone else, and he was handsome. Samuel worked with him and gave him precise instructions from God, but Saul's "obedience" was never as precise. Eventually God rejected Saul in favor of "a man after his own heart" (1 Samuel 13:14), but it would be a long and slow transition.

The Essential Story

How had it come to this? The king of Israel, disguised as a commoner, had skulked into Endor seeking help from a medium. Yet what else was he supposed to do? Samuel had stopped talking to Saul before he died, and God now refused to speak through prophets, dreams, or other means.

The medium was clearly suspicious of her nighttime visitor because she was breaking the law, but how could she know *he* was the one who had outlawed such occult activities back when he was in God's good graces?

Saul hadn't asked for the job. He'd gone out one day looking for his father's lost donkeys and then gone home as Israel's first king.

It was downright embarrassing when Samuel came to anoint him and he'd been found hiding. But he had accepted the responsibility. He'd saved a group of soldiers from being blinded by Ammonite soldiers, and he'd repeatedly fought the tenacious Philistines. He had undeniably felt the Spirit of God in his life then, but not for a long while now.

He supposed his decline had started that time Samuel told him to wait seven days so Samuel could make a sacrifice before Israel went to battle. But Samuel had taken his own sweet time as Philistines gathered around Saul, and his soldiers starting deserting. Saul had made the sacrifice himself (1 Samuel 13:8–15). And later, when Samuel told him to exact God's judgment on the Amalekites by destroying all their people and animals, Saul took it on himself to spare their king and the best of their flocks and herds (1 Samuel 15). In both cases, it was an executive decision that made perfect sense—to him, at least.

Now he found himself again threatened by Philistines, and he was desperate for advice wherever he could get it. He told the medium to summon Samuel for him. When she did, she let out a shriek. Was she expecting some kind of spirit but instead was confronted by the actual prophet? At any rate, she immediately realized Saul's identity, and she feared for her life.

Saul, however, was concerned only with what Samuel had to tell him. The news wasn't good. Because of Saul's disobedience, Israel would fall to the Philistines in the ensuing battle. Then Samuel added an ominous forecast: "And tomorrow you and your sons will be with me" (1 Samuel 28:19). Saul was shaken to his core. He fell to the ground, and the next day's events occurred just as Samuel had said they would. Israel would benefit, however, because Saul's death would at last pave the way for David to become king and unite the people as never before.

Essential Truth

The offenses we tend to consider "little" sins may still result in major consequences if we refuse to acknowledge and confess them.

David and Goliath

1 Samuel 17

The Story Continues . . .

The prophet Samuel had recently anointed a very young David to be the next king of Israel (to the chagrin of his seven older brothers). But Saul was still on the throne, and David's position changed little. He was relegated to the least desirable household chores, including shepherding and running errands.

The Essential Story

Some days just don't work out as expected. When David got up that morning, who knew he would find himself on a battlefield, striding directly toward the most enormous (and irate) human being he had ever seen?

He had been assigned the simplest of tasks: take some food to his big brothers in Saul's army along with a gift for their commander. They were doing the real work of fighting the Philistines while David served as message boy. But when David got to the camp, the two armies were in a cold war of sorts. The Philistines were on one hillside, the Israelites were on another, and a valley lay between them. David discovered, to his alarm, that a nine-and-a-half-foot behemoth named Goliath had been coming out twice a day for forty days, challenging the Israelites to send an opponent for a winner-take-all fight.

David's very appearance had sparked his brothers' resentment and anger, which they let him know in no uncertain terms, and volunteering to fight Goliath hadn't helped. King Saul was reluctant to send out someone so young and inexperienced, but after forty days he had few other options. Besides, David appeared surprisingly confident as he spoke of God's deliverance in his previous encounters with lions and bears. Saul offered his own armor for protection, but it was an uncomfortable fit, and David removed it. David also preferred his sling to any other weapon. He chose five stones; he would need only one. (A sling was an amazingly accurate weapon in the right hands [Judges 20:16].)

When Goliath saw that David was "little more than a boy" (1 Samuel 17:42), he was outraged that Israel hadn't sent out a more challenging opponent. He swore he would feed David's carcass to the birds, but David assured him it would be the other way around.

In addition to being such a sizeable human, Goliath also had the best possible protection and weaponry. The one exposed area was his forehead, and that was the target where David's stone landed dead center. The Philistine fell, and David used Goliath's own sword to cut off his head.

With the Philistine champion dead, the Israelite army surged with newfound courage. Saul's forces chased their enemies back to their cities and then looted their camp. David's heroic act earned him one of Saul's daughters for a wife and a tax exemption for his family. The citizens of Israel were soon singing his praises—literally. David's instant fame, however, would quickly generate major problems between him and Saul.

Essential Truth

Exciting things can happen when we give God control of each day's to-do list.

David and Bathsheba

2 Samuel 11–12

The Story Continues . . .

After David made an instant name for himself by defeating Goliath, he had to learn the tactics of politics, war, and diplomacy—quickly. Avoiding Saul's relentless pursuit after the king turned on him, he sometimes lived among the Philistines without either being killed or having to fight against his own people. When Saul finally died, David managed to unite his supporters with those who supported Saul, establishing Jerusalem as the nation's capital. The kingdom flourished. For the longest time it seemed he could do no wrong, but that time was about to run out.

The Essential Story

"You are the man!"

The truth of the prophet's accusation (2 Samuel 12:7) hit David like the rock he had used to floor Goliath. Nathan was clever. He had provoked David to outrage and condemnation toward someone for theft of a single sheep, when David himself was attempting to cover up adultery and murder.

He should have been in battle with his troops, but this time he had decided to stay home. He was cooling off on his roof and chanced to see a beautiful woman bathing in a nearby home. He could have left it at that, but he sent someone to find out who she was. She was Bathsheba, the wife of Uriah, one of David's soldiers. Despite this discovery, David sent for her and slept with her. He tried to leave it at that, but Bathsheba later sent word that she was pregnant. Her bath had been a ritual purification after menstruation, so the baby had to be David's.

But Uriah didn't know that. David immediately recalled him under the ruse of receiving a report about how the battle was going. David heard his report and then dismissed him, presuming he would go home to sleep with his wife. But Uriah was so conscientious that he considered himself still on duty, and he stayed with David's servants. David told him to stay two more days, during which David got Uriah drunk, but the devoted soldier still wouldn't go to his own house.

When nothing else worked, David decided to ensure Uriah would be killed. He sent him back to the battle to deliver a sealed note to the commander, ordering him to position Uriah in the most extreme fighting and to then have the other troops withdraw from him. Sure enough, Uriah was killed—and so were several other valiant men while following David's orders.

When Nathan showed up with a contrived story about a rich man with many flocks and herds who took away the one little ewe lamb a poor man possessed, David did not see the connection. But now he realized the fury he had felt toward the rich man was judgment on himself. Making the situation worse, Nathan said the child born of the affair would die. David fasted, wept, and prayed, but when the child died, he accepted it and moved on with his life.

David made no attempt to deny or excuse his actions, and he wrote an intimate psalm to confess his sin (Psalm 51). He and Bathsheba would have another child, Solomon, who would supersede David's older children and become heir to the throne. But David had to be concerned about Nathan's other warning: "Now, therefore, the sword will never depart from your house, because you despised [the Lord] and took the wife of Uriah the Hittite to be your own" (2 Samuel 12:10). Apparently, his grief was not over.

Essential Truth

Confession is the only way to deal with sin. Attempting to deny or downplay it only creates additional problems.

David and Absalom

2 Samuel 13–19

The Story Continues . . .

David's affair with Bathsheba was a turning point in David's life. Prior to that, no problem or situation seemed to defeat him. Afterward, however, very little went smoothly in his family life, and the resulting consequences affected the entire nation. Nathan's prophecy that the sword would never depart from David's house would be fulfilled quite literally.

The Essential Story

Before David became king, and as he spent months trying to avoid the wrath of King Saul, he was building a family as well as an army. His first six sons were born to six different women (2 Samuel 3:1–6), which created problems as they got older.

David's oldest son, Amnon, developed a sexual attraction to his stepsister, Tamar. Acting on his impulses was not only forbidden by law (Leviticus 18:9) but was just as socially unacceptable as it would be today. Yet urged on by a friend, he got her alone and raped her, ignoring her reasoned pleas to reconsider (2 Samuel 13:12–15). In a moment, Amnon's "love" for Tamar turned to hatred.

When David heard of the offense, he was furious, yet he said nothing to Amnon. Perhaps he was haunted by his own lack of self-control with Bathsheba. Tamar's full brother, Absalom, hated Amnon for what he'd done, but he didn't let his emotions show. He waited two years before he had his servants assassinate Amnon. Then he fled the country. David had dealt with Amnon's death, but he continued to mourn for Absalom.

David's commander, Joab, attempted to bring father and son back together, which turned out to be a terrible idea. No sooner had Absalom reconciled with David than he began a years-long campaign to take over the kingdom. He was a handsome and charismatic figure, and his hair was so thick that he lost about five pounds with each annual haircut.

As soon as David discovered Absalom's plans for an attempted coup, he fled Jerusalem to spare the city unnecessary damage. But he left behind some loyal friends to keep him informed and ten concubines to run the household. One of the first things Absalom did on his arrival in Jerusalem was to sleep with David's concubines in a rooftop tent so everyone could see who was the new boss. Then Absalom and his army went after David.

David, though, was experienced in warfare under such conditions. He divided his supporters into thirds and split up, but they were all commanded not to harm Absalom. The conflict took place in a heavily forested area, and Absalom's army took heavy losses—more from the terrain than from David's soldiers. One day Absalom himself was found dangling with his head (most likely his hair) stuck in an oak tree. The soldier who found him honored David's instructions, but Joab was incensed that he hadn't killed Absalom on the spot. Joab, acting on what he believed was best for the nation, personally thrust three javelins into Absalom's heart while he was still hanging there alive.

David was so distraught over Absalom's death that he couldn't even celebrate his victory and the deliverance of Jerusalem. Joab chided him for causing his people to slink back into the city rather than rejoicing. But one benefit of this civil war was that David discovered which of his friends could really be trusted and which ones couldn't. When he was very old and about to die, he designated Solomon as the next king and gave him an enemies list that included Joab and another of David's sons, Adonijah. The prophet Nathan had been right: Family conflicts plagued David until the very end of his life.

Essential Truth

Unconditional love for other people, including our children, doesn't include unconditional acceptance of their unrighteous, sinful behavior.

Solomon

1 Kings 3–11

The Story Continues . . .

Two of David's sons had made a play to usurp the kingdom, but David's choice for king was Solomon, the son he'd conceived with Bathsheba. Perhaps he hoped Solomon's life would atone for their first child, who had died as punishment for David's adultery and murder committed during his initial affair with Bathsheba. And indeed, Solomon was an unqualified success, almost to the very end.

The Essential Story

The people couldn't stop talking about their new king. One of his first rulings was to cut a baby in half! Of course, by giving the order, he clearly saw the panic of the real mother as she witnessed her child threatened, thus exposing the lies of the imposter. What wisdom!

Wisdom was the one thing Solomon had asked for when given the opportunity to request anything from God. He wanted to be a good leader, and he knew a king most needed "a discerning heart" able to distinguish between right and wrong (1 Kings 3:9). Since he hadn't asked for wealth or honor, God promised him those things as well, but his renown was the result of "wisdom" and "understanding" beyond measure (1 Kings 4:29).

David had fought the battles to bring peace to the area, and he'd wanted to build a permanent temple for God. But he was denied that privilege because of all the blood on his hands. That honor went to Solomon, and he spared no expense: olive and cedar wood, elaborate carvings, cut stone—and much of it overlaid with solid gold. (His own dwelling wasn't too shabby either.) At the dedication of the temple, God again appeared to Solomon, promising to establish his throne over Israel forever, with one condition: "if you walk before me faithfully with integrity of heart and uprightness, as David your father did" (1 Kings 9:4).

People who came to experience his wisdom also marveled at his wealth. One notable visitor was the Queen of Sheba, who came from Arabia and left "overwhelmed" by the things she saw and heard (1 Kings 10:5). She presumed everyone around Solomon must have been perpetually happy.

However, Solomon himself might not have agreed. He is generally accepted as the author of the book of Ecclesiastes, which details the writer's search for meaning in life. Among other things, he had tried wisdom, hedonistic pleasure, hard work, and wealth in a search for contentment. But he kept coming back to the fact that everyone dies in the end. All his work, wealth, and accomplishments would just go to someone else, eventually.

Solomon also pursued women; he accumulated seven hundred wives and three hundred concubines. Sadly, he allowed his many foreign wives to turn his attention to other gods. As a result, God did what he had said he would do: He brought the magnificent kingdom Solomon had created to an abrupt end. For David's sake, God waited until Solomon died, and he preserved the tribe of Judah for Solomon's son to rule. But the kingdom would remain divided, with separate kings and ongoing conflicts, until both Israel and Judah were defeated by outside forces and carried into exile.

Solomon had a life many of us can only dream of, and yet his story doesn't have a happy ending.

Essential Truth

Knowledge and God-given wisdom are tremendous assets, yet they are of little benefit if not put into practice.

Elijah on Mount Carmel

1 Kings 18–19

The Story Continues . . .

After Solomon's reign, the separate kingdoms of Israel and Judah each had a series of kings, but very few of them were godly—or even morally upright—leaders. When the rulers refused to seek God's leadership, God began to make known his will through prophets. Some simply spoke God's word boldly and faithfully. Others, like Elijah and Elisha, were given great power to emphasize the truth they proclaimed.

The Essential Story

"Hey! Shout louder! Maybe your god is busy thinking. Maybe he's traveling or asleep!"

Elijah was getting fed up with the foolishness of the priests of Baal, prompting his sarcasm. Since early that morning they'd been trying to evoke a response from their "god" through crying out, dancing, and even slashing themselves with swords and spears until blood gushed out. The people of Israel were watching and waiting as the priests tried to convince Baal to send fire from heaven to consume their sacrifice.

Elijah was waiting his turn. Until the day before, he had been a wanted fugitive. Three years ago he had introduced himself to King Ahab and pronounced God's judgment on Israel's sin: no rain until further notice. By now the resulting famine was severe, and Ahab hated him. But when Elijah said God was ready to send rain again, he had Ahab's attention. Elijah had told the king to assemble the people of Israel along with Queen Jezebel's priests on top of Mount Carmel. (Jezebel was a supporter of the 450 prophets of Baal and four hundred prophets of Asherah.) Outnumbered 850 to 1, it appeared that Elijah was the underdog in this "contest," yet he knew he represented the living God rather than an idol carved of wood or stone.

The bleeding and defeated priests finally gave up at midafternoon, their sacrifice untouched. As everyone watched, Elijah stepped up for his turn. First, he rebuilt an altar to God that had been demolished, using twelve stones to commemorate the tribes of Israel and the promises God had made to them. He dug a trench around the altar, placed wood on it, and laid out a bull that had been prepared for offering. Then he had the people fill four jars of water and douse the offering. He told them to do it again and then a third time. By then the wood was soaked and the trench filled with water.

Elijah then offered a short but very public prayer, asking God to make himself known so the people would turn back to him. At once fire fell from heaven and burned up not only the sacrifice but also the wood, the stones, the dirt underneath, and even the water in the trench. The Israelite onlookers immediately fell to the ground and worshiped God. Elijah told them to seize the prophets of Baal and not let any of them escape. He had them all put to death in accordance with the Mosaic law (Deuteronomy 13:1–5). Then he returned to the top of Mount Carmel and told Ahab to hurry home because rain was on the way.

Jezebel was none too happy, and Elijah found himself running for his life and even questioning his calling as a prophet. But God spoke to him and renewed his sense of purpose, and soon Elijah became a mentor to Elisha, another bold prophet of God.

Essential Truth

Those who stand boldly for God may frequently be outnumbered, but they will never be overcome.

Naboth's Vineyard

1 Kings 21

The Story Continues . . .

After Elijah's memorable demonstration of God's power on Mount Carmel, the people of Israel repented, but King Ahab and Queen Jezebel weren't changed in the least. Although they were supposed to be leading God's people, the story of Naboth's vineyard shows just how self-centered and spiritually bankrupt they had become.

The Essential Story

Israel had already endured a series of bad kings, but Ahab took despicable to a new level. Worse, he had married Jezebel, a queen of equally low, if not lower, standards. They seemed to feed off each other's wickedness. Scripture makes it clear: "There was never anyone like Ahab, who sold himself to do evil in the eyes of the Lord, urged on by Jezebel his wife" (1 Kings 21:25).

Ahab's sins were not just against God but against anyone who got in his way. He had found a piece of land near his palace that he wanted to use for a vegetable garden. It currently was a vineyard owned by a man named Naboth. Ahab offered to give Naboth a better vineyard or to buy the property from him outright, but Naboth refused because it was a family inheritance.

After Naboth's refusal, Ahab was pouting around his palace, sulking in bed, and refusing to eat. Jezebel told him to act more like a king and said she would take care of the problem. She sent out letters under Ahab's name to the leaders of Naboth's city, telling them to proclaim a day of fasting and to make sure Naboth was out in public. They were also to hire a couple of "scoundrels" to falsely testify that Naboth had cursed both God and King Ahab (1 Kings 21:10). On their testimony, Naboth was found guilty and stoned to death.

Problem solved, or so they thought. Jezebel told Ahab to get up and go take possession of his new vineyard. But God sent Elijah to meet Ahab in the vineyard, and Elijah accused Ahab of theft and murder. As a result of such egregious sin (and a lifetime of similar actions), Elijah declared that dogs would lick up Ahab's blood and would devour Jezebel. This was not merely a metaphorical judgment; it would be fulfilled literally. Ahab would eventually die in battle (1 Kings 22:29–40), Jezebel would be thrown to her death by her own staff (2 Kings 9:30–37), and dogs were involved in both instances.

Ahab was replaced as king by Ahaziah, his son, who "served and worshiped Baal and aroused the anger of the Lord, the God of Israel, just as his father had done" (1 Kings 22:53). And so the series of worthless kings of Israel continued.

Essential Truth

God's judgment of sin is not always immediate, but unless repentance is offered, judgment is certain.

Naaman Visits Elisha

2 Kings 5

The Story Continues . . .

After a lifetime of faithful service, Elijah had been taken to heaven in a whirlwind amid horses and chariots of fire, apparently without dying (2 Kings 2). His prophetic role was taken over by his trainee, Elisha. God worked through both men to perform incredible feats, including resurrecting someone from the dead (1 Kings 17:17–24; 2 Kings 4:18–37). During a time when so many kings of Israel were self-serving, Elijah and Elisha both made sure to give God the credit for the works they did.

The Essential Story

When Naaman showed up unexpectedly to see the king of Israel, the king couldn't help but notice the 750 pounds of silver, the 150 pounds of gold, and the ten sets of new clothes he was offering. But the letter he was carrying had the king concerned—even fearful. The king of Syria wanted him to cure this guy of his leprosy?!

Naaman explained that his wife had a servant girl who had been taken during a previous Syrian raid on Israel. The girl was confident that a prophet in Israel could take care of Naaman's problem. She had told her mistress, who had told her husband, who had told the king of Syria, who had made this strange request of the king of Israel.

Syria and Israel had been in an on-again, off-again war, so the Israelite king feared this was a ploy to resume the conflict. What was *he* supposed to do about some stranger's case of leprosy? He tore his clothes in distress and confusion. But when Elisha heard what had happened, he sent word for the king to send Naaman to him.

Naaman went on to Elisha's house with an entourage of servants, horses, and chariots, but the prophet didn't even go out to meet him. He sent a messenger telling Naaman to go wash in the Jordan River seven times, and his disease would be cured.

Naaman became peeved and surly. He had expected to see Israel's great prophet come out, wave his hand, and cure him. He muttered that the rivers in Syria were much better, so why was he sent to the Jordan? However, his servants reasoned with him that if Elisha had given him a difficult assignment, wouldn't he have done it? He went to the Jordan, dipped into the water seven times, and came up with pure, clean skin.

He was an instant convert: "Now I know that there is no God in all the world except in Israel" (2 Kings 5:15). Naaman even requested a load of Israelite soil so he could build an altar when he got home and continue to worship God. He wanted to give Elisha a gift, but the prophet refused. Receiving payment would suggest that the prophet was responsible for the healing rather than God. The two men parted on good terms.

In an addendum to this story, Elisha had a servant named Gehazi who saw an opportunity to turn a quick profit—or so he thought. He waited until Naaman was a distance away, and then he caught up with him, telling him that two new prophets had just arrived and that he was requesting silver and clothes for them. Naaman was more than willing to give what he asked and more. Gehazi hid his ill-gotten gain, but he soon discovered that Elisha somehow knew exactly what he had done. The prophet wasn't happy. Because of Gehazi's deceit, he acquired leprosy for the rest of his life.

Essential Truth

Willingness to provide spiritual healing or comfort should transcend political, social, and other barriers.

The Fiery Furnace

Daniel 1; 3

The Story Continues . . .

After the kingdom was divided following the rule of Solomon and split into the nations of Israel and Judah, that breach was never repaired. Both nations had a long series of kings, very few of whom had the slightest interest in what God desired for the people. God began to send prophets to warn the people. If they didn't improve, they would be captured by their enemies and taken into exile. They didn't improve. Assyria conquered Israel in 722 BC. Judah fell to Babylon in 586 BC.

The Essential Story

They had never felt more conspicuous. With an entire nation on its knees before King Nebuchadnezzar's ninety-foot-tall gold image, three standing figures couldn't help but draw attention. Hananiah, Mishael, and Azariah realized their stay in Babylon had gone as well as could be expected—so far. Along with Daniel, they had undergone the king's three-year training period for the best and the brightest and had come out on top. They didn't care much for their assigned Babylonian names—Shadrach, Meshach, and Abednego—but they didn't have a choice about that.

They did have a choice about whether to bow before the king's image. It had been made perfectly clear that anyone who refused to do so would be thrown into a raging, fiery furnace. This was their first real test of faith, but they were still standing.

Their rivals were quick to tell on them. Nebuchadnezzar was angry to hear of their defiance, but he was willing to give them a second chance. They told him not to bother, that they not only trusted their God to deliver them but that they trusted him even if he chose *not* to deliver them.

Nebuchadnezzar's demeanor changed immediately. On this day of dedication, he was supposed to be the center of attention, but he had just been relegated to second place by these young men. He furiously commanded that the furnace be heated seven times hotter than usual, had the three tied up, and then ordered them thrown in. The intensity of the heat killed the soldiers who tossed them in, so Nebuchadnezzar was astounded to see Shadrach, Meshach, and Abednego walking around in the flames. Not only that, but he also saw a fourth figure. He approached the door of the furnace and called for them to come out.

The huge crowd assembled to submit to a golden image instead witnessed the three Hebrew youths emerge from the furnace. They were no longer bound, and they showed no hint of fire damage. Neither their hair nor clothing had been singed, and they didn't even smell of smoke. Nebuchadnezzar was so impressed that, on the spot, he passed a law forbidding anyone to say anything bad about the God of Shadrach, Meshach, and Abednego, under penalty of death. In addition, the three received a promotion.

Two questions frequently arise from this story. First, where was Daniel? We aren't told, but surely he wasn't present. (He would have his own test of faith soon enough.) And second, who was the fourth figure in the fire? Because this was such a miraculous event, the best guess is that God sent an angel, or perhaps it was even a Christophany—an appearance of Christ—in the Old Testament. Like many other unexplained accounts in Scripture, we can only speculate as we do our best to understand the wonders of God in our world.

Essential Truth

God may not always deliver his people from physical harm when they make a stand for him, but he always rewards their faith.

Daniel in the Lions' Den

Daniel 6

The Story Continues . . .

During his lifetime in Babylon, Daniel proved useful to several kings. He interpreted dreams for Nebuchadnezzar (Daniel 2; 4) and read the mysterious handwriting on the wall for Belshazzar (Daniel 5), which predicted Babylon's fall to the Persian Empire. The new Persian king was Darius, and he held equally high esteem for Daniel, although Daniel was not without his detractors.

The Essential Story

Darius had been up all night, pacing and fasting. How could he have been so stupid? He should have seen through their ploy when that bunch of self-seeking officials came to him with an irrevocable injunction, declaring that for thirty days no one in the kingdom could ask anything of any god or of any man other than Darius. He had played right into their hands, and he took little consolation in realizing it certainly wasn't the first time a group of sycophants had gained what they wanted by playing to a king's ego.

They knew he was about to promote Daniel over the rest of them. Daniel deserved it, without a doubt. He did no wrong and always had a spirit about him that set him apart from the rest. The others knew Daniel wouldn't stop praying to his God just because a governmental document forbade it, so they had written the punishment into the official decree: Offenders would be cast into a den of lions.

Darius had signed the document one day, and then in no time they were back with charges against Daniel. Darius was trapped. He could neither change the law nor reduce the consequences of disobeying it. He had looked for loopholes all day, but when evening came, he reluctantly ordered Daniel thrown into the lions' den. Although the rest of the kingdom was prohibited from making such a request, Darius asked Daniel's God to deliver him. Then he spent a restless night hoping for . . . what? A miracle?

At the first light of day, the king hurried to the lions' den and called for Daniel, although his anguished voice belied any expectation of an answer. But Daniel responded, and he assured Darius that God had sent an angel to shut the mouths of the lions. When Daniel was released, Darius issued a new worldwide proclamation in every language, ordering everyone to show proper respect for the God of Daniel.

Those who had plotted against Daniel had drawn Darius into their conspiracy, causing him great consternation. Persian kings weren't known for their forgiving natures. Darius ordered that the conspirators, along with their wives and children, be dropped into the lions' den. With the lions' mouths no longer closed, they were dead before they hit the floor.

Essential Truth

Sometimes God's law must supersede civil law, but believers can still attempt to bring God's wisdom to their secular peers and leaders with courage and humility.

The Call of Isaiah

Isaiah 6; 38; 2 Kings 20:1–11

The Story Continues . . .

As God prepared to send his people into exile, he first sent prophets to explain what was about to happen and why. Theirs was often a difficult job because the people were generally resistant to their message. Several prophets recorded their initial calling from God along with an accompanying vision of his glory—evidence of the significance of their message and a reminder of the importance of their work.

The Essential Story

Isaiah was on his way to see Hezekiah, one of the few decent kings who had ever ruled over Judah. The two of them had been through a lot together, including a frightening encounter with Sennacherib, a ruthless Assyrian leader who intended to conquer Judah. Isaiah kept Hezekiah encouraged with God's assurance that all would be well. The problem was resolved with divine intervention—an angel of the Lord had killed 185,000 Assyrians in a single night. Sennacherib was forced to go back home, where he was soon assassinated by his own sons (2 Kings 18–19).

This time Isaiah's message to Hezekiah was not at all comforting: "Put your house in order, because you are going to die; you will not recover" (2 Kings 20:1). Hezekiah immediately began to pray and weep, and God heard him. Isaiah had not even left the king's court before God told him to go back with a new message: God had heard Hezekiah and would add fifteen years to his life. The sun had just cast a shadow that had crept down a nearby stairway, so as a sign of assurance to Hezekiah, God had the shadow reverse its course.

Isaiah's faithfulness as a prophet was driven by his initial vision of God about forty years earlier. He saw God, enthroned and worshiped by six-winged angels. The heavenly temple was filled with smoke and shook at the sound of the angelic voices. In the presence of such holiness, Isaiah was painfully aware of his sinfulness. He proclaimed, "Woe to me! . . . I am ruined! For I am a man of unclean lips, and I live among a people of unclean lips, and my eyes have seen the King, the Lord Almighty" (Isaiah 6:5). In response, one of the angels took a live coal from the altar and touched it to Isaiah's lips, declaring his guilt removed and his sin atoned for. When he heard the Lord ask, "Whom shall I send? And who will go for us?" Isaiah was ready to respond, "Here am I. Send me!" (v. 8).

Isaiah accepted his calling from God and never looked back. His work and writing were influential. Among other insights, he foresaw a "suffering servant" of God in passages we connect with the mission of Jesus Christ. Other than Psalms, his book is the Old Testament work most quoted in the New Testament.

Essential Truth

No one can properly represent God until God prepares them for service.

Jeremiah in the Pit

Jeremiah 36–38

The Story Continues . . .

In contrast to Isaiah, who revealed very little about his personal life and received little if any resistance to his messages, Jeremiah was both descriptive about his personal ordeals and a regular target of scorn. His message was that Jerusalem was about to fall, and the people's best option was to go willingly to Babylon as captives. (It would have prevented the destruction of their city.) But that wasn't news anyone wanted to hear, and Jeremiah suffered for it.

The Essential Story

From the bottom of the cistern, Jeremiah could see just a small circle of sky. He had to wonder if that would be the last thing he ever saw. Thankfully, no water was left. He wouldn't drown, but the remaining mud was thick, and he sank into it—a miserable experience. The officials who had lowered him into the makeshift holding cell had sought his death, and King Zedekiah had left the sentencing up to them. They had no plans to return.

Zedekiah wasn't the first king who had refused to listen to Jeremiah. When Jehoiakim was king, Jeremiah had taken great pains to record God's message to the nation on a scroll. (More accurately, he had dictated the message while his secretary, Baruch, had written it down.) When the scroll was read in the presence of the people in the temple and to the king's officials, they had become alarmed. But when it was read to the king, Jehoiakim showed absolutely no remorse or repentance. As each section of the scroll was read, he used a knife to cut it off and burn it as fuel, piece by piece until it was all gone. While in hiding from the king, Jeremiah had once more dictated the message from God, and Baruch faithfully wrote it all down again. Jehoiakim's stubborn refusal to respond to God's message had consequences: He would die without having a son succeed him as king, and he would not receive a proper burial.

Zedekiah wasn't listening to Jeremiah either, but he wasn't quite as antagonistic. When a compassionate servant approached the king, asking permission to rescue Jeremiah, Zedekiah okayed his request. The servant even brought rags for Jeremiah to put in his armpits to prevent rope burn as he was pulled out.

Jeremiah was free, but Judah's time was up. Just as God had said, Babylon overtook the city. Zedekiah tried to run, but he didn't get far. Nebuchadnezzar made him watch as the Babylonians slaughtered his sons, and then Zedekiah was blinded and forced to live with that final image the rest of his life. It was a low point in Israel's history, but those who heeded Jeremiah's message could take comfort that it would not be permanent. After seventy years of exile, God would bring his people home again (Jeremiah 25:8–14).

Essential Truth

When people oppose God, they're also likely to reject those who attempt to proclaim God's word.

Ezekiel and the Valley of Dry Bones

Ezekiel 37:1–14

The Story Continues . . .

Ezekiel was a temple priest and prophet and among the first group of Israelites exiled to Babylon. From Babylon, he prophesied the fall of Jerusalem, yet after the destruction of the city he assured his people of God's intent to see them through the ordeal and eventually release them.

The Essential Story

The Jewish captives in Babylon must have lost all hope as reports arrived from their homeland that the walls, city, and temple had all been destroyed. Ezekiel was called to ensure that they didn't lose hope or faith in God.

Like Isaiah, Ezekiel had a specific calling from God, with visions of heavenly creatures and activities (Ezekiel 1:1–24). His visions continued throughout his ministry, both to encourage him personally and to demonstrate what God had in store for Israel. But for a group that tended to be glum and morose because of their circumstances (Psalm 137:1), probably nothing would have inspired them more than Ezekiel's vision of a valley of dry bones.

God showed Ezekiel a valley filled with many bones, all of them "very dry," and asked, "Can these bones live?" Anyone's instinctive response would be, "No way!" but Ezekiel was tactful enough to reply, "Sovereign Lord, you alone know" (Ezekiel 37:2–3).

God instructed Ezekiel to prophesy to the bones, telling them to feel the breath of God, grow flesh and skin, and live. Ezekiel did as he was told, and sure enough, the bones rattled together into connected skeletons on which grew tendons, flesh, and skin. It was surely an amazing sight, yet they had no breath. God told Ezekiel to prophesy again, calling for breath to enter the bodies and enable them to live. Once more, Ezekiel followed instructions, and the "vast army" came to life and stood on their feet (v. 10).

God explained that the bones represented the people of Israel who thought they were beyond help and hope. Ezekiel was sent to encourage and comfort them. They were to prepare to receive the Spirit of God, find new life, and return to their own land. It seemed like an impossible feat, but when it happened, they would realize that God had spoken and acted.

Essential Truth

No matter how bleak your situation appears, God can resolve the problem and empower you to experience new life.

Hosea and Gomer

Hosea 1–3

The Story Continues . . .

In addition to speaking for God, the prophets were sometimes instructed to do something that served as an object lesson, visually illustrating God's message. Ezekiel, for example, had been told to build a miniature city under siege to represent the destruction of Jerusalem and then to symbolically bear God's punishment on the people (Ezekiel 4:1–8). But perhaps no prophet was given a more peculiar—or heartbreaking—assignment than Hosea.

The Essential Story

Hosea had heard God clearly, yet he was still trying to make sense of the command: "Go, marry a promiscuous woman and have children with her" (Hosea 1:2). Israel had many pure and virtuous women for a man who wanted to get married, but God made his purpose clear: He wanted to show the people that, "like an adulterous wife this land is guilty of unfaithfulness to the Lord" (v. 2).

Oh well. Hosea arranged to marry a woman named Gomer and hoped for the best. They soon had a child together. God would name all of Hosea's children. This first one, Jezreel ("God sows"), appeared to denote a location where God would judge Israel for sinful offenses in the past, although names for future children would be much more specific and personal.

Gomer's second child was a daughter to be named Lo-Ruhamah ("Not loved"), because God was about to suspend his protective love for Israel and allow them to be conquered by the Assyrians. Judah, however, would be spared for a while. If Hosea had suspicions about the paternity of this daughter, his concerns were most likely confirmed when Gomer had a third child, a son God named Lo-Ammi ("Not my people").

The relevance of Gomer's wandering desires became clear in God's prophetic message to Hosea. God compared Israel to an unrepentant adulterous wife who is called into account. When she ran out of other options and wanted to return to her "husband," God would not be quick to take her back. Israel's "adultery" was spiritual; deserting the Lord to get involved with worship of the Baals was no small indiscretion. Still, in time God would take back his misguided and unfaithful people. He would eventually show love to "Not loved" and would again claim those he had designated as "Not my people."

To demonstrate the significance of his great mercy and forgiveness, God instructed Hosea to reclaim his wife, who by this time had fallen into some sort of servitude. Hosea had to buy her back at the cost of a common slave. We can only imagine what kind of whispers, jeers, and condescending looks he must have endured in his male-dominated society. Yet Hosea, as much as anyone, learned to identify with the pain God feels when the people he loves are quick to desert him.

Essential Truth

Although forgiveness and redemption are among the many gifts God bestows on the people he loves, he's saddened by the sin that necessitates such gifts.

Jonah

Jonah 1–4

The Story Continues . . .

Like Hosea, Jonah was one of twelve "minor" prophets in Scripture—not a measure of importance but rather of the length of their writing. And like Hosea, Jonah was a prophet sent to Israel rather than to Judah. But all things considered, Jonah was probably least like all the other prophets, which is what makes his story so intriguing.

The Essential Story

Jonah was sailing west—with the full knowledge that God had sent him to Assyria, overland to the *east*. He was about to discover that no matter how far or fast you go, you can't escape an omnipresent God.

God sent a storm so violent that it threatened to break the ship apart. The trained sailors were frightened and crying out to their gods, and they advised the sleeping Jonah to wake up and do the same. Then they cast lots to determine who was responsible for such divine wrath, and Jonah's name came up. He admitted he was the cause and told them to throw him into the sea. The sailors did all they could to avoid that option, but out of desperation they finally did as he said. As Jonah sank into the water, the sea immediately became calm.

God sent a "huge fish" to swallow Jonah. He spent three days and nights in its belly, which provided ample time for him to pray and recommit to obey God. When the fish vomited Jonah onto dry land, he was ready to head for Nineveh, Assyria's capital city (where Mosul, Iraq, is today). After he arrived, he proclaimed God's message that Nineveh would be destroyed in forty days. But he wasn't ready for their response.

The Ninevites believed God. The king declared a total fast and period of repentance. God relented of his intent to destroy the city, and it was a happy ending for everyone—except Jonah. The prophet hadn't been afraid the Ninevites wouldn't listen to him; he'd been afraid they *would*. In his estimation, these cruel enemies of Israel didn't deserve God's mercy, which he let God know in no uncertain terms. He even challenged God to take his life.

Jonah was holding out for some kind of judgment on the city, so he camped out for a while to see what might happen. God sent a plant to grow quickly to provide much-welcomed shade for Jonah. But the next day God sent a worm to wither the plant, followed by blazing sunshine and a scorching hot wind. Again, Jonah wished for death, but God was trying to teach him something: "You have been concerned about this plant, though you did not tend it or make it grow. It sprang up overnight and died overnight. And should I not have concern for the great city of Nineveh, in which there are more than a hundred and twenty thousand people who cannot tell their right hand from their left—and also many animals?" (Jonah 4:10–11).

The question is left unanswered, hanging there for all of us to consider. Do we get so caught up in our petty comforts and selfish desires that we miss the bigger picture of God's mercy taking place all around us?

Nineveh's reprieve was short-lived. Years later the prophet Nahum would pronounce God's sure and certain judgment on the Assyrian Empire and its proud capital city. But the fact that they responded to Jonah's message demonstrates the power of repentance. Whether Jonah learned that lesson is uncertain.

Essential Truth

The messages of God are often just as significant for the messenger as they are for the designated recipient—if not more.

Esther

> **Esther 1–10**

The Story Continues . . .

The Jewish citizens of Judah had been defeated by (and many of them deported to) Babylon. But in time, the Babylonians fell to the Persian Empire, leaving the Jews still in captivity yet under new overseers. Esther was one young Jewish girl who was persuaded to make the most of an opportunity while in exile, and her decision to do so resulted in her saving her entire people. Although the book of Esther makes no direct mention of God, it's a fascinating, page-turning piece of literature that repeatedly demonstrates the benefits of being in the right place at the right time, by divine design.

The Essential Story

Esther wasn't sure her cousin Mordecai really knew what he was asking of her, but she knew she had to do it. After raising her like a parent and prompting her to become Xerxes' new queen, he would not ask such a favor if it weren't necessary. Beauty would take her only so far; this situation required courage.

Mordecai had warned her not to reveal her nationality, and now she saw why. After Mordecai refused to bow down to Haman, the king's second-in-command, it wasn't enough for Haman to punish Mordecai. In retaliation, Haman paid a lot of money to persuade King Xerxes to send letters across the land, instructing local officials to annihilate *all* Jews, regardless of age or gender, on a specific day. (Mordecai's feud with Haman did not extend to King Xerxes. In fact, Mordecai had foiled an assassination plot and saved the king's life. The event was recorded, but nothing had been done to reward him—yet.)

Mordecai wanted Esther to intercede with Xerxes, but she had no regular access to the king. Anyone who approached him in his inner court uninvited would be put to death unless the king was in a favorable mood and held out his golden scepter. It had been a month since Esther had been summoned, and Xerxes' former queen had only recently been summarily divorced and deposed for a minor infraction. This was no small favor her cousin was asking, yet any reluctance Esther felt was overruled by Mordecai's logic: "Who knows but that you have come to your royal position for such a time as this?" (Esther 4:14).

Esther, along with all the Jews in Susa, fasted and prayed for three days. She then approached the king, who was glad to see her. Rather than frantically pouring out her request, however, she simply asked Xerxes if she could host a dinner for Haman. He quickly agreed. Haman was elated when he heard of this invitation. He went home and boasted of his special relationship with the king and queen, although Mordecai's continued lack of respect irked him to no end. When his friends and family suggested he have a gallows pole constructed for Mordecai's execution, he did so at once.

It just so happened that Xerxes couldn't sleep that night and was reading some recent history. He came across the record of Mordecai's exposure of the assassination plot and discovered that nothing had been done to reward him. Haman arrived at that moment in the outer court to ask Xerxes for permission to hang Mordecai. Before he could make his request, Xerxes asked him, "What should be done for the man the king delights to honor?" (Esther 6:6).

Haman naturally assumed *he* was the man the king delighted to honor, so he piled on the rewards and accolades: some of the king's finest robes, one of the royal horses to ride, a royal crown, and a palace official to lead him through town proclaiming the king's favor. Xerxes liked the idea, and he told the bewildered and aghast Haman to go do all those things for Mordecai. The proud Haman could hardly bear the shame of honoring his nemesis, but at least he had his special party to look forward to.

Esther entertained Xerxes and Haman for an entire day. On the second day, Xerxes finally got around to asking her what she wanted from him. She explained that someone in the kingdom had arranged to have her and all her people not merely sold as slaves (which would have profited the king) but annihilated. When Xerxes asked who it was, she replied, "An adversary and enemy! This vile Haman!" (Esther 7:6).

Enraged, Xerxes stormed out of the room to compose himself while Haman stayed to beg Esther's mercy. She was reclining on a couch, and as he fell at her feet, perhaps reaching out to appeal to her, Xerxes returned and misread the situation: "Will he even molest the queen while she is with me in the house?" (v. 8). A helpful servant mentioned to the king that Haman had a new gallows pole in his yard, and Xerxes commanded that Haman be executed on it. (Most "hangings" in the Old Testament were probably references to impaling the convicted on a sharpened pole.)

New letters were immediately sent out to revoke Haman's death orders. The Jews were not only spared, but they even were given the authority to defend and destroy others, like Haman, who continued to be a threat to them. The annual celebration of Purim continues until this day, to commemorate this dramatic deliverance of the Jewish people.

Essential Truth

God sometimes places specific people in specific places for specific reasons.

Nehemiah Rebuilds the Walls of Jerusalem

Nehemiah 1:1–7:4

The Story Continues . . .

While Esther ruled as queen, exiled Jews were returning to their homeland in waves. A large group returned first with Zerubbabel in 538 BC to rebuild the temple in Jerusalem (Ezra 1–6). A second group returned in 458 BC with Ezra the priest, who went to prepare the people spiritually and deal with inappropriate behavior among some of the other priests (Ezra 7–10). Nehemiah led a third group in 444 BC.

The Essential Story

Nehemiah had asked for this job, and he was committed to seeing it through, but he was beginning to see why so many of his people had preferred to stay in the comfort of the Persian Empire rather than returning to their ramshackle homeland. Even with the improvements made in repairing the temple, his brother's description of the "great trouble and disgrace" (Nehemiah 1:3) in the city had been no exaggeration. It had convinced him to ask his boss, King Artaxerxes (the son of Xerxes), for extended time off to supervise the rebuilding of Jerusalem's walls. As the cupbearer to the king, Nehemiah was a trustworthy servant Artaxerxes would miss, but the king didn't want to see his companion looking so forlorn.

When Nehemiah arrived in Jerusalem and told the people what he intended to do, he met immediate resistance, especially from three local officials, but many others responded and got to work. At the halfway point, the resistance intensified from verbal insults to physical threats. Nehemiah decided to take both spiritual and practical precautions: "We prayed to our God and posted a guard day and night to meet this threat" (Nehemiah 4:9). The workers took turns working construction and standing guard, and they kept their weapons close.

Then Nehemiah's enemies conspired against him personally, using various strategies: trying to lure him away from Jerusalem, falsely accusing him of wanting to become king, and hiring a false prophet to persuade him to take refuge in the temple from a supposed plot, which would have discredited his reputation since Nehemiah wasn't a priest. With prayer and discernment, Nehemiah saw through all their ruses.

Despite all the attempted interference, rebuilding the walls took only fifty-two days. Their success was a clear indication to their enemies that God was at work. Ezra read the law to the people, who wept as they listened. But Ezra and Nehemiah assured them this was a time for joy, and they encouraged the people to celebrate. At long last, proper worship of God was restored in Jerusalem.

Essential Truth

People working for God can expect opposition, but they can also expect God's support and provision to be far greater than any opponents.

STORIES OF JESUS

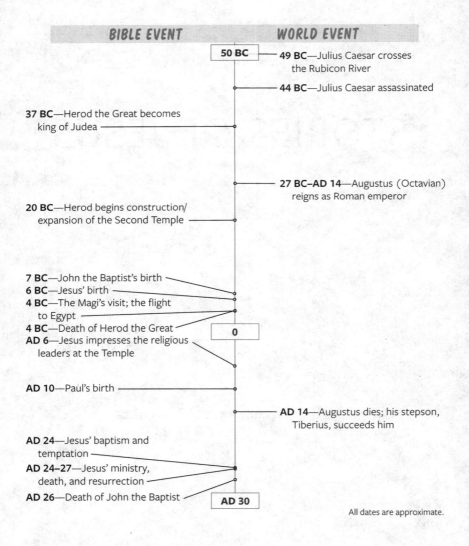

BIBLE EVENT	WORLD EVENT

50 BC

49 BC—Julius Caesar crosses the Rubicon River

44 BC—Julius Caesar assassinated

37 BC—Herod the Great becomes king of Judea

27 BC–AD 14—Augustus (Octavian) reigns as Roman emperor

20 BC—Herod begins construction/ expansion of the Second Temple

7 BC—John the Baptist's birth
6 BC—Jesus' birth
4 BC—The Magi's visit; the flight to Egypt
4 BC—Death of Herod the Great
AD 6—Jesus impresses the religious leaders at the Temple

0

AD 10—Paul's birth

AD 14—Augustus dies; his stepson, Tiberius, succeeds him

AD 24—Jesus' baptism and temptation
AD 24–27—Jesus' ministry, death, and resurrection
AD 26—Death of John the Baptist

AD 30

All dates are approximate.

The Birth of John the Baptist

The Story Continues . . .

During the four hundred years or so that passed between the two Testaments of Scripture, the Jewish people (after release from exile) tried to rebuild and reestablish their nation. They had survived the spread of the Greek Empire even though Antiochus IV Epiphanes had tried to do away with their culture altogether. Now in subjection to the Roman Empire, they had limited freedom and were kept on a short leash. Many Jewish people were looking for their prophesied Messiah, but first a forerunner would prepare the way.

The Essential Story

Most people their age had grandchildren already, yet Zechariah kept praying for a child. Childlessness in first-century Israel was a pitiable condition. He had no direct line of succession to whom he could pass along his legacy, and he knew it pained his wife, Elizabeth, to hear her friends speak of their large families. Even worse, some people would have presumed that one or both of them must have committed a sin for which God was punishing them.

Yet he and Elizabeth remained steadfastly devoted to God. Zechariah enjoyed serving as a priest, and tonight he had the rare honor of being chosen by lot to burn incense in the Holy Place of the temple while many others were praying outside. It was in that solitude that Zechariah had a life-changing encounter. The angel Gabriel appeared beside the altar of incense, frightening Zechariah. But Gabriel had good news: Elizabeth was going to have a child—a special child at that!

They were to name the boy John and prepare him from birth to be a servant of God. He would have the spirit and power of Elijah and would pave the way for the coming of the Lord. Zechariah asked for a sign, but that was the last thing he would verbally request for nine months. Because of his doubt, his sign would be his inability to speak until the child was born.

After it became obvious to those outside that Zechariah was taking far too long to light some incense, they grew concerned. When he emerged and was mute, they were amazed as he did his best to pantomime what had happened to him.

Just as Gabriel had said, Elizabeth became pregnant and chose to go into seclusion for several months. Mary, a relative, went to visit her then, during her own miracle pregnancy. Mary's initial greeting caused Elizabeth to be filled with the Holy Spirit, and Elizabeth's baby "leaped in her womb" (Luke 1:41). Mary responded with a memorable song of praise to God. They encouraged one another for three months before Mary went back home.

In time, Elizabeth gave birth to her son. Friends and relatives presumed she would name him after Zechariah or someone else in the family, but she insisted on the name John. They asked Zechariah for verification, and as soon as he wrote "His name is John" (Luke 1:63), he regained his speech. Clearly God was at work in this family, and lest there be any doubt, Zechariah immediately delivered a prophetic song of praise to God that included a declaration of what the child would accomplish.

John grew into a fearless prophet, boldly declaring the truth of God and Jesus (Luke 3:1–22). He was eventually put to death by Herod, after which Jesus gave him high praise (Luke 7:28).

Essential Truth

Faithfulness while waiting for God to act produces the best results.

The Birth of Jesus

Matthew 1:18–2:23; Luke 1:26–2:38

The Story Continues . . .

Israel's prophets had long ago foretold the coming of a Messiah, a Savior of the nation. The time had come at last, but the event was unlike anything anyone had anticipated.

The Essential Story

It was the first deep sadness Mary had felt for two years or so. She and Joseph were almost to Egypt, recently forced to flee Judea in the middle of the night to escape Herod's violent jealousy and paranoia. As she cradled her new child in her arms, she had already begun to hear stories of mass execution of male children in Bethlehem.

She had been doing much thinking lately. The truth was she had hardly stopped pondering ever since the angel Gabriel appeared that night in Nazareth with the startling news. How could a virgin have a baby? What did it mean that her child would be "the Son of the Most High" (Luke 1:32)? What would she say to Joseph?

Joseph didn't understand, of course. He planned to break their engagement, even though he agreed not to make her a public spectacle. But an angel appeared to him to change his mind. He also told Joseph to name the baby *Jesus* "because he will save his people from their sins" (Matthew 1:21).

Mary's trip with Joseph to Bethlehem for the government-mandated census had not been easy on her. It was disappointing to find no available rooms upon their arrival. And it had been more than a little alarming to deliver her baby that very night, among the haystacks. But those little inconveniences were quickly forgotten when she saw the face of her child.

Time moved quickly from that point. Almost immediately a group of shepherds appeared, excitedly telling of a sky full of angels who had pointed them to the manger. They left spreading the word and amazing everyone with what they had experienced.

A few days later, when Mary took Jesus for his purification rites, she encountered two unusual people who gave her more to ponder. One was an eighty-four-year-old widow named Anna, who never left the temple. Anna immediately thanked God for Mary's child and started talking about him to "all who were looking forward to the redemption of Jerusalem" (Luke 2:38). The other person was an old man named Simeon, who said he had been promised that he would see "the Lord's Messiah" before he died (v. 26). He praised God that Jesus was "a light for revelation to the Gentiles, and the glory of your people Israel" (v. 32). Yet he also warned Mary that because of the destiny of the child, "a sword will pierce your own soul too" (v. 35).

Eventually Mary and Joseph found a house to stay in for a while, where they had a visit from wise and wealthy magi who had followed a star from the East, bringing gifts of gold, frankincense, and myrrh. Unwittingly, the magi had asked Herod for directions to find "the one who has been born king of the Jews" (Matthew 2:2), alerting Herod to a potential threat he then determined to eliminate. Angels advised the magi to take a different route home, and Joseph was warned in a dream to go immediately to Egypt and wait. When the magi failed to report back, Herod ordered the deaths of all male children under two years of age. Only after Herod's death was it safe to return to Nazareth, where the family led a normal life—at least, as normal as possible for parents of a child who had already been identified as the Son of God and Savior of the world.

Essential Truth

From his birth, Jesus has been a perpetual source of promise and hope for all kinds of people—rich and poor, young and old, faithful and adversarial. Those who respond to him in faith find forgiveness, love, and new life.

Jesus' Baptism and Temptation

Matthew 3:1–4:11

The Story Continues . . .

Very little is known about Jesus' early life. After a couple of birth accounts and one short look at how his twelve-year-old mind was already special (Luke 2:41–52), Scripture picks up with his public ministry at age thirty—the age at which Old Testament priests could begin serving (Numbers 4:1–3). Jesus was still an unknown, but his cousin, John the Baptist, was beginning to attract a lot of attention.

The Essential Story

It was time. Jesus stood at the edge of the crowd gathered to hear John preach. John didn't speak in the temple or synagogues; he spoke boldly in the wilderness of the need for repentance and spiritual integrity, and people were flocking to hear him. Truth be told, some of them were probably more interested in seeing him than listening to him. Dressed in a camel's-hair shirt and leather belt, and dining on locusts and wild honey, he evoked the image of a prophet from long ago in Israel's history. Little did they know yet that John was the "Elijah" prophesied by Malachi, who would precede the arrival of the day of the Lord (Malachi 4:5–6). Yes, it was time.

Jesus stepped forward to be baptized. When John saw who it was, he resisted, explaining that their roles should be reversed. But Jesus insisted, and John baptized him. As Jesus left the water, the physical presence of the Holy Spirit alit on him, and a voice from heaven declared, "This is my Son, whom I love; with him I am well pleased" (Matthew 3:17).

Yet immediately after such an affirming moment, the Spirit led Jesus into the wilderness, where he fasted for forty days and nights and then was tempted by the devil. Clearly Jesus was hungry, so the devil tempted Jesus to turn stones to bread. Jesus answered with a quote from the Mosaic law: "Man shall not live on bread alone, but on every word that comes from the mouth of God" (Matthew 4:4).

The devil tried again, this time quoting Scripture while tempting Jesus to throw himself down from the highest point of the temple and be rescued by angels, thereby attracting instant fame. Once more Jesus cited the law: "Do not put the Lord your God to the test" (v. 7).

In a last-ditch effort, the devil showed Jesus the splendor of all the kingdoms of the world and promised he could have it all—if only he would bow down and worship him. For the third time, Jesus quoted Deuteronomy and dismissed his tempter: "Away from me, Satan! For it is written: 'Worship the Lord your God, and serve him only'" (v. 10).

At that point angels arrived to attend to Jesus, and the devil left him alone . . . for now (v. 11).

Essential Truth

Jesus faced all the temptations we face, but he did not sin, and therefore he is qualified to help us through our own temptations (Hebrews 2:18; 4:15).

Jesus Turns Water into Wine

John 2:1–11

The Story Continues . . .

After Jesus' baptism and temptation, he began to teach in the synagogues and soon collected a following of disciples. After a night of prayer, he designated twelve of them as apostles and began to spend more time with them (Luke 6:12–16). Not the most prominent members of their society, they were fishermen, a tax collector, a Zealot (a member of a group promoting the overthrow of Rome), and other ordinary people. But what they would see and receive from Jesus over the next three years would transform most of them into strong pillars of faith and founders of a whole new religion, beginning with what they witnessed at a wedding in Cana.

The Essential Story

Jesus wished his mother wouldn't be quite so presumptuous. Mary, Jesus, and his disciples were among the guests at a wedding when word circulated that the hosts had run out of wine—an unforgettable if not unforgivable breach of hospitality that would shed great embarrassment on the newlyweds. Mary looked at Jesus and said, simply, "They have no more wine" (John 2:3).

This was more than a statement of fact. Jesus knew she was really saying, "Do something." He told her it was not yet time for him to demonstrate all he could do, but surely his heart went out to the young couple. He determined that he could work with the servants behind the scenes to alleviate a potentially shameful situation.

Nearby were six jars used for ceremonial washing, each large enough to hold twenty to thirty gallons. Jesus told the servants to fill them with water, which they did. He then told them to take a sample to "the master of the banquet" (v. 8). When the wedding emcee tasted it, it was fine wine. He pulled aside the groom and wanted to know why he had waited to bring out the choice wine; it was standard procedure to start with the best and save the cheaper wine until later, when the guests would be less likely to notice.

Not many of the guests that day knew what had happened, but the servants did. Jesus had performed an effortless transformation of water to wine, impressive in both quantity and quality. More importantly, his new disciples saw what he'd done and believed in him. This would be the first of many miracles Jesus performed to confirm he was sent from God and was truly who he would claim to be—the Son of God and Savior of the world.

Essential Truth

Jesus' compassion toward us goes beyond spiritual concerns, applying to physical, emotional, and other aspects of life as well.

Nicodemus Visits Jesus

John 3:1–15

The Story Continues . . .

From the beginning of his ministry, Jesus faced resistance from the scribes, Pharisees, and Sadducees—various religious leaders of the Jews. They were threatened by his interpretation of the Law, which varied from theirs in significant ways, and perhaps they were even more alarmed at his instant popularity with the people. His teaching and miracles drew huge crowds, and public debate sometimes became confrontational. Battle lines were being drawn, with Jesus and his followers on one side and the traditional Jewish leaders on the other. But there were exceptions.

The Essential Story

This new rabbi fascinated him, and Nicodemus wanted to learn more about him. He went to see him at night. For one thing, the crowds had dispersed, so perhaps the two of them could have a private conversation. And for another, if he were spotted, it might be hard to explain why a Pharisee was breaking ranks to get to know Jesus better.

After Jesus welcomed him, Nicodemus opened with a compliment: "Rabbi, we know that you are a teacher who has come from God. For no one could perform the signs you are doing if God were not with him" (John 3:2). But Jesus' response mystified him: "Very truly I tell you, no one can see the kingdom of God unless they are born again" (v. 3).

Nicodemus was confused, the result of thinking too literally. Jesus went on to explain that genuine worship and maturity are spiritual issues—a fact many of Israel's teachers (the Pharisees) seemed to be missing. They were inarguably experts on the *written* Law of Moses, but they were missing the guidance of God's Spirit, which Jesus compared to the unseen wind. (The same Hebrew word could be interpreted "wind," "breath," or "spirit.")

The only response Nicodemus could come up with was "How can this be?" (v. 9). Jesus continued to explain about himself and God's plan of salvation. And as Jesus kept talking, he spoke the words that are among the most quoted in all of Scripture: "God so loved the world that he gave his one and only Son, that whoever believes in him shall not perish but have eternal life" (v. 16).

Nicodemus's questions were simplistic—some might say downright foolish. But because he kept querying and seeking to understand, Jesus revealed deep truths about God that millions of people have cherished in the centuries since they were first spoken.

Did Nicodemus understand enough to make a difference? It seems so. He's mentioned twice more in Scripture. One time as the religious leaders were debating what to do about Jesus and many of them wanted to arrest him to keep him quiet, Nicodemus reminded them that Jesus had the right to a trial (John 7:45–52). Even more importantly, Nicodemus accompanied Joseph of Arimathea—another Pharisee—to anoint Jesus' body and bury him after his crucifixion (John 19:38–42). His nighttime conversation with Jesus appears to have left a lasting impression.

Essential Truth

God welcomes all questions intended to bring us closer to him, even if they seem foolish or uninformed.

Jesus and the Woman at the Well

John 4:4–42

The Story Continues . . .

When the northern kingdom of Israel fell, many of the Jewish people were carried off to Assyria (1 Chronicles 5:26). In time, some of those who remained intermarried with the occupying Assyrians. Their descendants, known as Samaritans, had long been detested by the Jews for compromising their ethnic and religious heritage. By the time Jesus arrived, the centuries-long antagonism between full-blood Jews and Samaritans had escalated into bitter hatred. Conscientious Jews would go well out of their way to avoid even setting foot in Samaria—usually.

The Essential Story

She made her way to the well at noon, like always. She preferred to avoid the accusing eyes of the other women of her community who typically did that chore in the cool of the morning. But today she had a worse problem: a Jewish *man* sat beside the well. Maybe he would ignore her, let her get her water, and leave. But she was expecting a nasty comment, at best.

What she didn't expect was a request: "Will you give me a drink?" (John 4:7).

Clearly, this guy didn't know proper social protocol. She explained that Jewish men simply didn't ask Samaritan women for favors. Again, his statement surprised her: "If you knew the gift of God and who it is that asks you for a drink, you would have asked him and he would have given you living water" (v. 10).

She was curious but skeptical. "Living water" sounded intriguing, yet he had no bucket, no ladle, no drinking vessel. She asked for his credentials. After all, this well dated back to the patriarch Jacob, and she was proud of it.

He didn't seem impressed. He told her, "Everyone who drinks this water will be thirsty again, but whoever drinks the water I give them will never thirst. Indeed, the water I give them will become in them a spring of water welling up to eternal life" (vv. 13–14).

The more this man spoke, the more she wanted to hear. He told her to go get her husband, and when she explained she wasn't married, she learned he already knew she'd been through five husbands and was living with still another man. Yet his tone wasn't accusatory.

She gave him credit for being a prophet, but he seemed to be more. She mentioned worship, and his views on the subject were insightful, inspiring, and refreshingly different from anything she had ever heard—especially from a Jewish authority. She cautiously expressed her belief in a promised Messiah who would, like this stranger, explain everything to her people. She probably hadn't dared to hope so much, but he responded, "I, the one speaking to you—I am he" (v. 26).

Just when the conversation had reached a peak, the disciples returned from town, where they had gone for food. They realized they had walked in on something, and they didn't dare ask questions, but the woman used their arrival to excuse herself and go gather other Samaritans. She told them the man at the well knew everything she had ever done and persuaded them to come listen to this stranger. *Could he really be the Messiah?*

The people were responsive to Jesus and urged him to stay a while. He remained with them two days, and many of them became convinced that "this man really [was] the Savior of the world" (v. 42). For those Samaritans and others, the fact that God's salvation would not be exclusively for the Jewish people was tremendously good news.

Essential Truth

Even though Jesus knows things about us we'd rather no one knew, he offers love, forgiveness, and new life.

Proof of Jesus' Authority to Forgive

Mark 2:1–12

The Story Continues . . .

As Jesus began his ministry, he quickly attracted large crowds for two main reasons: (1) his teachings were different from anything the people were accustomed to, yet authoritative, and (2) the people's desire to witness or receive a miraculous healing. The traditional religious leaders, who were concerned about all the attention he was receiving, criticized him on both counts.

The Essential Story

They were too late! The house was already packed. The five men had come as soon as they heard Jesus had returned to his home base of Capernaum, but by the time they got there, the crowd was spilling out of the house. They couldn't even get near the door, especially since four of them were carrying the fifth on a mat.

But they had promised their paralyzed friend they would take him to Jesus, so they came up with another plan. They found the outside stairway and carried him up to the flat roof. Then they removed some of the baked mud tiles and carefully lowered their friend down to Jesus, where he immediately became the center of attention.

Jesus was first to respond. When he saw the man, he spoke, fondly: "Son, your sins are forgiven" (Mark 2:5).

What? That was all well and good, but it wasn't why they carried the guy across town. He desperately wanted to walk! What were they going to do now? But then Jesus spoke again. He appeared to be addressing a group of frowning scribes: "Why are you thinking these things? Which is easier: to say to this paralyzed man, 'Your sins are forgiven,' or to say, 'Get up, take your mat and walk'?" (vv. 8–9).

The four friends wondered what the scribes had been thinking— and how Jesus could have known. Everyone knew only God could forgive sins, but any charlatan could *say* a person's sins were forgiven. Were they doubting his word?

Jesus made everything clear with his next comment: "I want you to know that the Son of Man has authority on earth to forgive sins" (v. 10). Turning to their friend, he said, "I tell you, get up, take your mat and go home" (v. 11).

Their friend stood! Then he rolled up his mat and made his way through the dense crowd as a buzz of praise and amazement filled the room. It was proof enough for most of those present that Jesus displayed the power of God. Many of the religious leaders, however, would never be convinced.

Essential Truth

Jesus' miracles were not merely a show of power but authentication that what he tells us about God is trustworthy.

Jesus Feeds Five Thousand (and Later Four Thousand)

Matthew 14:13–21; 15:29–39; John 6:1–14

The Story Continues . . .

As stories about Jesus continued to spread throughout the land, it became harder and harder for him to find time to himself. He had just received word about John the Baptist's death, and he tried to retreat to a quiet place. But people continued to follow him. He felt compassion for them, and before long a crowd of thousands had assembled. That presented his disciples with a challenge as evening fell.

The Essential Story

It was exciting to be around Jesus. You never knew what you might see as people came from far and near to be healed. They would be moaning and crying in pain, and then, after seeing Jesus, they'd be laughing and rejoicing. Lame people started walking. Blind people began to see. The young boy could watch all day, and evidently a lot of other people could too. But why hadn't anyone else thought to bring a snack?

The sun was starting to set, and the boy was just getting ready to eat the dinner he'd brought, when one of Jesus' disciples, named Andrew, asked if he could have it. The boy had overheard the disciples talking about how Jesus expected them to provide food for the crowd. It seemed they were hoping to round up enough to prepare a meal.

He'd been willing to share, as he'd been taught to do, but it looked as if his two fish and five small barley rolls were all they collected. It was a paltry amount that wouldn't have been a big meal for him alone, much less for this crowd of thousands. The disciples seemed a little panicky, but Jesus was calm. He had everyone sit down on the grass, and he then said a prayer. Then he started breaking up the food and giving it to his disciples, telling them to hand it out to the people. He invited everyone to eat as much as they wanted, and as he kept breaking, the food kept coming.

The boy was astounded to see his meal somehow feed five thousand full-grown men, along with all the women and children there. There were even leftovers! The disciples gathered up twelve baskets of food after everyone was full. He supposed that would be their lunch tomorrow.

It felt good to contribute something Jesus could use. He could really learn to like a rabbi like Jesus, who cared about little things like providing dinner when people were hungry as much as he cared about healing them when they were sick. It must be the best job ever to be one of Jesus' disciples. If Jesus did things like this every day, their faith must be strong!

Unfortunately, the disciples apparently didn't learn much from this experience. As we see in Matthew 15:29–39, a short while after this gathering Jesus gave them another opportunity to feed a crowd. Yet they were just as helpless as before, even with a little more food and not quite as many people. Jesus repeated the miracle and fed four thousand men, plus women and children, with seven loaves and a few fish.

Essential Truth

When you offer God what little you have, he ensures you will have more than enough.

Two Miracles on the Sea

Matthew 14:22–33; Mark 4:35–41

The Story Continues . . .

Many of Jesus' miracles were public, performed amid great crowds. Others, however, were witnessed by only a few people. Two remarkable events took place on the Sea of Galilee as Jesus and his disciples were crossing in a boat. Sea travel was not only convenient and saved time; it also allowed Jesus to devote more focused attention to his closest friends.

The Essential Story

The enormous crowd was dispersing, everyone filled with fish and bread and still marveling at how effortlessly Jesus had fed them all. Jesus, eager to spend some time alone talking to his Father, sent his disciples ahead of him in a boat. Then he climbed the mountain to pray alone.

It wasn't a good night for sailing. The disciples battled the wind for hours, into the early morning. Already exhausted, they grew downright terrified when they saw a form approaching their boat across the water. They thought it was a ghost. But before they could identify the figure, they recognized the voice. Jesus assured them, "Take courage! It is I. Don't be afraid" (Matthew 14:27).

Peter, always the impulsive one in the group, wanted proof. He immediately offered, "Lord, if it's you . . . tell me to come to you on the water" (v. 28). Jesus told him to come on. Peter began to walk across the water toward Jesus, and only then, it seems, did he think about what he was doing. He started to focus on the wind more than on his Master, and then he began to sink. Jesus reached out and kept him from going under, gently chastising Peter for his shortage of faith—even though it must have been clear to the other disciples that at least Peter had left the boat!

As soon as Peter and Jesus climbed into the boat, the sea grew still again. The disciples responded with immediate praise, saying, "Truly you are the Son of God" (v. 33).

On another occasion, Jesus was sailing *with* the disciples. He was exhausted, and he had fallen fast asleep on a cushion in the stern. Because of the geography of the area, the Sea of Galilee is prone to sudden strong storms, and a fierce one arose that day. Even though at least four of the disciples were experienced fishermen, they all feared for their lives as the boat filled with water. In desperation, they woke Jesus with a question that sounded like an accusation: "Teacher, don't you care if we drown?" (Mark 4:38).

Before he responded to the disciples, Jesus spoke to the wind and waves: "Quiet! Be still!" (v. 39). The wind stopped instantly, and the sea grew calm. No longer afraid of the storm, the twelve became terrified for another reason. They asked one another, "Who is this? Even the wind and the waves obey him!" (v. 41).

Jesus again challenged them to increase their faith. After all, he must have wondered what they were *expecting* him to do when they woke him up.

Essential Truth

On occasion, Jesus demonstrated complete authority over the power of nature, which challenged the faith of even those closest to him.

Jesus' Authority over Evil Spirits

Mark 5:1–20

The Story Continues . . .

While many people sought Jesus' healing for physical problems (leprosy, paralysis, bleeding diseases, and so on), he healed others whose problems clearly had a spiritual source: evil spirits. One of the most extreme cases took place in the Gentile territory of the Gerasenes.

The Essential Story

As their boat went ashore on the other side of the Sea of Galilee, the disciples were still amazed at how Jesus had stopped a violent and life-threatening windstorm simply by speaking to it. But no sooner had they landed than they were approached by a naked man coming from a group of tombs. As he got closer, they could tell he was disheveled, had a crazed look, and was bleeding from apparently self-inflicted wounds. Even more frightening, he made a beeline for them and threw himself down at Jesus' feet.

They would discover the man had a longstanding reputation in the area. He was uncontrollable. People had repeatedly tried binding him with chains and foot irons, but he broke through them all. Every attempt to subdue him had been futile. He lived in the tombs, where he would wail and cut himself with stones.

Jesus discerned the problem and told an impure spirit to come out of the man, but he was met with resistance. The spirit spoke from within the man: "What do you want with me, Jesus, Son of the Most High God? In God's name don't torture me!" (Mark 5:7).

Jesus asked the spirit's name. He replied, "My name is Legion . . . for we are many" (v. 9). Then he repeatedly begged Jesus not to send them away.

Jesus' disciples, already rattled from their terrifying experience on the sea, must have become even more thunderstruck. This evil spirit was surely an overwhelming force. A legion was the largest division of the Roman army, numbering as many as six thousand men. Yet not only did this "legion" of spirits recognize Jesus, but they also submitted to him. They acknowledged his authority and tried to negotiate with him, first imploring him not to send them away and then requesting to at least be allowed to go into a nearby herd of two thousand pigs.

Jesus granted their second request, but then the pigs at once ran into the sea and drowned. The men tending the pigs ran into town, and word spread quickly. People flocked to see for themselves what they had been told. They came looking for the spectacle of thousands of drowned pigs, but they also witnessed an even greater sight: The crazy naked man from the tombs was dressed, sitting calmly, and coherent.

The power Jesus had demonstrated struck fear into the entire community, and they begged him to leave. The cleansed man pleaded to go with Jesus, but Jesus convinced him to stay. As he returned to normal life, he would be a regular reminder of the day Jesus had visited and displayed the unlimited power and mercy of God.

Essential Truth

Although evil exists in today's world, the power of God keeps it in check and will someday do away with it forever.

Jesus' Transfiguration

Matthew 17:1–13; Luke 9:28–36

The Story Continues . . .

At the height of Jesus' popularity with the people and his many miracles, he began to prepare his disciples for his death. His power and fame led to increasing opposition from the established religious leaders, which he knew would eventually affect his followers as well. His disciples were slow to comprehend what he was saying, so in addition to telling them what to expect, he also showed them something they would never forget.

The Essential Story

Peter was thrilled to be included in Jesus' "inner circle" once more. Jesus had started spending more time with just Peter, James, and John, and today he had invited the three of them to go up on a mountain to pray with him. Just days before, he had asked the twelve their opinions about who he was, and Peter had boldly responded that Jesus was the Christ—the Messiah who had been prophesied and Son of the living God. His impulsive answers weren't always correct, but he had been right on target that day, and it had felt good to receive Jesus' praise. Yet Jesus had warned them all not to share that information with anyone outside their group.

When the four of them finished their climb, Jesus began to pray. Peter and his two friends were weary and drifting off to sleep. But they became "fully awake" when they realized what was happening. Jesus' clothing was as bright as a flash of lightning and the "appearance of his face [had] changed" (Luke 9:29). He was conversing with two other figures: Moses and Elijah! They had been discussing Jesus' forthcoming death, and they were preparing to leave.

Peter quickly spoke up, offering to build three tents: one each for Jesus, Moses, and Elijah. Perhaps he wanted the heavenly visitors to stay a bit longer, or maybe he just wanted to commemorate the event, but he was silenced when a cloud surrounded them and a voice from the cloud said, "This is my Son, whom I have chosen; listen to him" (v. 35).

Oops. Once again, he had spoken too soon. He had been wrong to equate Moses and Elijah with Jesus. Even though they were consummate representatives of the law and the prophets, Jesus was greater. When they heard the voice, he and James and John fell prostrate to the ground. When he looked up again, only Jesus was there. Jesus calmed his three disciples and instructed them not to tell anyone what they had seen until after his resurrection.

This event would leave a lasting impression on Peter. Years later, when he was a church official writing letters to encourage other believers, he was still as excited to have been an eyewitness of Jesus' "majesty" as he'd been that day on the mountaintop (2 Peter 1:16–18).

Essential Truth

Jesus was fully human, yet he was also fully God, as he demonstrated on rare occasions.

Jesus and the Woman Caught in Adultery

John 8:1–11

The Story Continues . . .

Jesus' increasing popularity was becoming a growing irritation to the scribes and Pharisees, the established religious leaders of Israel. They were trying numerous strategies to force him to say something for which they could bring a formal charge and silence him. This incident demonstrates just how low they would go in their efforts to entrap him.

The Essential Story

Two people in the crowd were the objects of unsought attention. One of them desperately didn't want to be there—the sole woman in this group had been caught in the act of adultery and dragged through the streets by men who'd already judged her guilty without the benefit of a trial. Now they sought an immediate death sentence, and she was surely frightened. (She had to wonder where the man also caught in the act was. How could *he* have escaped?) She felt shame and embarrassment as well, not only from having her affair publicized but because, most likely, she was in some state of undress. These were not men patient to have given her adequate time to properly clothe herself.

The angry mob had rushed the woman directly from her bed to Jesus—the other party who found himself on the spot. He was teaching in the temple, so he and the woman were amid a large audience, forced to deal publicly with what was a sensitive matter.

The woman's accusers were quick to quote the law. Moses had been clear: "If a man commits adultery with another man's wife . . . both the adulterer and the adulteress are to be put to death"

(Leviticus 20:10). They turned the spotlight on Jesus, and in front of the assembled crowd they asked him if he agreed with Moses.

The religious authorities thought they had him. If he said no, he would be contradicting sacred Jewish Scripture and they could press formal charges. But if he said yes, his harsh judgment of this clearly vulnerable woman would surely taint his teachings about love and forgiveness. Theirs was a well-thought-out plot.

Instead of answering, Jesus stooped and wrote on the ground with his finger. His action has prompted much speculation as to what he was writing. The names of some of the Pharisees' paramours? Other specific sins of the scribes? Perhaps he was simply diverting his eyes from a scantily clad woman or writing his "new commandment" of love with the finger of God, as the original Ten Commandments had been written. No one knows for sure, but it doesn't matter.

What does matter is Jesus' answer when the Pharisees insisted that he respond. He looked up and said, "Let any one of you who is without sin be the first to throw a stone at her" (John 8:7). Then he returned to his writing. He didn't vote to absolve the woman, as if her sin didn't matter. But neither did he condemn her on the spot without giving her the opportunity to seek forgiveness. Her sin was evident, yet after being forced to think about it, everyone in the crowd had to admit that they had sins of their own. The accusers soon dispersed "one at a time, the older ones first" (v. 9). The next time Jesus looked up, only the woman remained.

He told her, "Neither do I condemn you." But he cared too much for her to leave it at that, so he also cautioned her to "go now and leave your life of sin" (v. 11)—not so much to avoid any further legal and spiritual trouble but because he knew that was what was best for her. He forgave her, and she was no longer subject to the scorn of the Pharisees. Jesus, however, couldn't say the same.

Essential Truth

Sin separates people from God and can result in spiritual death (Romans 6:23), but repentance and a commitment to Jesus restores the broken relationship and brings life.

The Parable of the Prodigal Son

Luke 15:11–32

The Story Continues . . .

Along with Jesus' interpretation of Scripture and straightforward teachings, he used lots of parables. A parable served to make a point without Jesus having to make a direct accusation that might have created unnecessary trouble for him. For example, one time when the religious leaders were grumbling about Jesus' associations with "sinners," he told three consecutive parables with the same theme (Luke 15). His story of a lost sheep and a lost coin were well received, but his listeners couldn't have missed his intent as he told this now-classic parable of a lost son.

The Essential Story

"There was a man who had two sons" (Luke 15:11).

Jesus had everyone's attention from the first sentence. The Jewish emphasis on family, especially sons, was a universal topic of discussion. And when the story continued with a disagreement about an inheritance, his listeners' interest was surely piqued.

The younger son brashly and prematurely requested his share of the inheritance, a grave social offense. It was akin to telling his father, "I wish you would go ahead and die," and yet the father granted the boy's request.

With all that wealth in hand, it didn't take long for the youngster to seek greener pastures. He left home for a distant country, where he "squandered his wealth in wild living" (v. 13). He went from riches to rags as, just when he had spent everything, a famine hit. The only job he could get was feeding pigs. (On hearing this, Jesus' listeners probably shuddered. This was a shameful and unclean job for any Jewish person.)

When the boy realized the pigs were eating better than he was, he "came to his senses" (v. 17). It was time for humility and repentance. He headed home, practicing his speech along the way. He would apologize, acknowledge his sin against God and his father, and ask to become a servant. Even then he would receive much better treatment from his father than he'd experienced out in the world.

His approach was tentative, but his father appeared to be looking for him. Even while he was far away, he saw his father running toward him. (More uncomfortable squirming from Jesus' listeners. It wasn't an attractive or appropriate sight for a full-grown male to hike up the hems of his robes and take off running.) Filled with compassion, the father couldn't wait to hug and kiss his returning son.

The boy began his speech, but the father wouldn't even let him finish; the lad's contrition was evident. The father ordered servants to provide him with a ring and a robe and to kill a fattened calf for a feast. A great celebration began.

Had Jesus concluded the parable there, it would appear to be a happy ending. Yet he continued, detailing how the older brother heard the music and dancing and asked what was going on. When he was told, he vehemently refused to participate. The father came out to beg him to join the celebration, but he was bitter and jealous: "Look! All these years I've been slaving for you and never disobeyed your orders. Yet you never gave me even a young goat so I could celebrate with my friends. But when this son of yours who has squandered your property with prostitutes comes home, you kill the fattened calf for him!" (vv. 29–30).

The father assured the older son, saying, "Everything I have is yours" (v. 31), but the son refused to be consoled. It wasn't enough for him to have his father's love if the younger (and less obedient) son had it too.

The tax collectors and sinners among Jesus' listeners would have found this parable most comforting, but the Pharisees and scribes would have bristled, realizing they were "the older brother." They didn't even want to acknowledge brotherhood with the other group, much less rejoice in the others' acceptance by God the Father. They could do nothing to change the ending of the story, but they could—and would—take out their frustration on the storyteller.

Essential Truth

As much as God hates sin, he rejoices when sinners repent and discover the loving relationship he wants to have with them.

The Parable of the Good Samaritan

Luke 10:25–37

The Story Continues . . .

If the Pharisees and other religious leaders took offense at Jesus' story of the prodigal son, his parable of the good Samaritan would have caused them even greater consternation. In this case, one of the leaders thought he was challenging Jesus, but then he discovered the opposite was true. Jesus' use of storytelling was so powerful that this parable completely redefined one of the most hurtful and hateful epithets of the first century.

The Essential Story

Having heard of Jesus' knowledge and how he sometimes interpreted Mosaic law in unusual ways, the lawyer had come to listen to him. He was an expert in Mosaic law too, and he decided to publicly test Jesus: "Teacher . . . what must I do to inherit eternal life?" (Luke 10:25).

Jesus answered, essentially, "You tell me."

No problem. The lawyer was up to the task. He quoted Deuteronomy and Leviticus as he replied, "'Love the Lord your God with all your heart and with all your soul and with all your mind'; and 'Love your neighbor as yourself'" (v. 27).

Jesus agreed with his answer but then added, "Do this and you will live" (v. 28).

No. That was too easy. The lawyer wanted to hear more from this upstart rabbi, and he wanted to justify himself. He asked, "And who is my neighbor?" (v. 29).

Jesus answered with one of his stories. He told of a Jewish man who was headed to Jericho on a rapidly descending road that had a reputation for dangerous thieves. Robbers left the man stripped, beaten, and almost dead. But wait. A priest was coming down the same road, yet he crossed to the other side and ignored the man.

The lawyer could explain that, given a chance. Perhaps the priest presumed the man was dead and didn't want to touch him, which would have ceremonially defiled him and kept him out of service for a while. Maybe he feared the robbers were still around. Maybe he thought the guy might be a robber himself, faking an injury. But Jesus didn't pause to allow the lawyer to comment.

Next, Jesus said, came a Levite down the road. (Priests were descendants of Aaron; Levites were descendants of Levi who assisted priests with their temple duties.) The Levite also crossed the road to avoid the injured man.

The lawyer could guess what was coming next. A regular Jewish guy was going to come along and show up the ones who considered themselves ministers. But no. Jesus' listeners probably responded with audible gasps when he told them the next traveler who approached the injured man was a *Samaritan*. The very word was essentially an expletive. The prejudice and hatred most Jews felt toward Samaritans for their mixed Jewish and Gentile bloodline was widespread. Had the roles been reversed, no self-respecting Jew would deign to stop and help an injured Samaritan.

Yet the Samaritan's care for the injured man was abundant and heartfelt. He treated and then bandaged the man's wounds. He put the man on his own donkey and led him to an inn, where he cared for him further. The next day he paid the innkeeper to watch the man until he could return, and he promised to reimburse him for any expenses.

The lawyer had started with a question for Jesus, and Jesus concluded his story with a question for the lawyer: "Which of these three do you think was a neighbor to the man who fell into the hands of robbers?" (v. 36).

The lawyer who had looked for loopholes to justify himself could find none. He couldn't bring himself to say the word *Samaritan*, but he responded, "The one who had mercy on him." Jesus told him to "go and do likewise" (v. 37).

In a single, short story, Jesus had not only removed all boundaries to the concept of "neighbor"; he had also demonstrated that knowledge of the Law was not enough, that God expected action. The lawyer surely wanted to object, but he had learned his lesson. He made no further comment.

Essential Truth

By vastly expanding our concept of "neighbor," Jesus challenges us to greater levels of commitment to love and serve others.

The Rich Man and Lazarus

Luke 16:19–31

The Story Continues . . .

In a culture often coldly characterized by the slogan "He who dies with the most toys wins," this story from Jesus offers a different perspective. Some people have questioned whether this is indeed a parable; if so, it's the only one where Jesus used a specific name. Regardless, his point comes through loud and clear, whether today or in first-century Israel.

The Essential Story

Jesus was teaching the crowds, using parables, stories, and fresh insights into their written law. He had just taught that no one can serve two masters—that it was impossible to serve both God and money. Among his listeners was a group of Pharisees who were ridiculing him because they had a well-established reputation for being lovers of money (Luke 16:14). His next story was primarily for their benefit, but it was relevant to all his listeners.

He told of a rich man who had the finest clothes and feasted on sumptuous foods every day. The man had learned to ignore a beggar at his gate named Lazarus, who was so covered with sores that he attracted wild dogs. Lazarus would gladly have taken any crumbs from the rich man's table, yet we see no hint that the man made any effort to help him.

Jesus said nothing about a burial when Lazarus died. Instead he was carried by angels to Abraham's side. The rich man also died eventually and did have a burial, and no doubt he had an extravagant funeral. But in the afterlife, he found himself in Hades, conscious and in agony from the fire but unable to do anything about it. He asked Abraham to send Lazarus with a drop or two of water to cool his tongue, but Abraham explained that a chasm had been positioned between Paradise and Hades that was impossible to cross. Besides, said Abraham, the rich man had never looked beyond his own comfort in life to help people like Lazarus. Now the tables were turned.

The rich man seemed to accept Abraham's reasoning, but he made another request: "Send Lazarus to my family, for I have five brothers. Let him warn them, so that they will not also come to this place of torment" (vv. 27–28).

Abraham replied that written Scripture—Moses and the Prophets—was available to them. God's truth was clear, and no one who ignored it could be persuaded by even a visit from someone returning from the dead.

Jesus provided no further commentary on this story, but no "lover of money" could miss the point. Whether his listeners wanted to interpret what he'd told them as literal or metaphorical, Jesus had made it clear, as he frequently did, that the next move was up to them.

Essential Truth

The character qualities and behaviors we choose for ourselves can have eternal significance—for better or for worse.

The Resurrection of Lazarus

John 11

The Story Continues . . .

Jesus' many miracles had already included at least two resurrections from the dead. One time he walked up on the funeral procession for a man who was the only son of his widowed mother.

Jesus had compassion and brought the man back to life (Luke 7:11–17). Later he restored to life the twelve-year-old (and only) daughter of a synagogue official named Jairus (Luke 8:41–42, 49–56). His third known resurrection miracle was much more personal and poignant, and it was a foreshadowing of his own pending resurrection.

The Essential Story

Where *was* he? Martha was fretting, as she was prone to do. She and her sister Mary had sent word to Jesus days ago that their brother Lazarus (not the same Lazarus from Jesus' story in Luke 16) was gravely ill. Now Lazarus had died and was buried. The mourners had arrived, but Jesus was not there to grieve with his friends. What could be keeping him?

Lazarus had been in his tomb four days when Martha finally got word that Jesus was approaching. When she went out to meet him, he was with his disciples, who looked a little uncomfortable. On their latest visit to Judea, the Jewish leaders had tried to both arrest and kill Jesus (John 10:31, 39). Jesus had delayed his return for a couple of days, but he had come back willingly, fully aware of the danger. Martha attempted to mitigate her disappointment: "Lord, . . . if you had been here, my brother would not have died. But I know that even now God will give you whatever you ask" (John 11:21–22).

Jesus assured her, "Your brother will rise again" (v. 23), but she thought he was referring to the final resurrection the Jews anticipated after death. Jesus told her, "I am the resurrection and the life. The one who believes in me will live, even though they die; and whoever lives by believing in me will never die" (vv. 25–26). She believed that Jesus was the Messiah and Son of God, yet she had no idea what he was planning to do.

Martha then ran to get Mary, who had a similar conversation with Jesus. Other mourners had followed Mary from the house, all weeping. Jesus asked where Lazarus was laid, and when they showed him, he wept as well.

As the crowd was discussing what might have happened if Jesus had been there earlier, Jesus told them to remove the large stone from the entrance to the tomb. Martha protested, concerned about the potential stench, but Jesus told her to stand by and watch for the glory of God. He said a prayer and then called loudly, "Lazarus, come out!" (v. 43).

It was a struggle for a man whose hands, feet, and head were all wrapped with cloth, but Lazarus did his best to walk out of his tomb. Jesus told the astounded onlookers to unbind him and let him go.

For many who had had doubts about Jesus until now, the resurrection of Lazarus was a turning point. Lazarus began to attract large crowds of people just as Jesus did, and many of them put their faith in Jesus. Consequently, the chief priests, who were already plotting to kill Jesus, started making plans to get rid of Lazarus (John 12:9–11). Whether the plot against Lazarus was carried out is unknown; this is the last he's mentioned in Scripture. The Bible's focus now shifts to Jesus, whose time on earth is growing short.

Essential Truth

If we believe that Jesus has absolute power over death, such belief can both console our sorrow when loved ones die and minimize our fear as our own death approaches.

Jesus' Triumphal Entry into Jerusalem

Matthew 21:1–11; Luke 19:28–40

The Story Continues . . .

After the resurrection of Lazarus, the religious leaders' efforts to quiet Jesus took on a new intensity. They feared that the people's growing devotion to Christ would bring down the wrath of Rome on them all. Caiaphas, the high priest, convinced them that "it is better for you that one man die for the people than that the whole nation perish" (John 11:50). But before they found a good opportunity to do away with Jesus, he had one shining moment when the crowds expressed the praise he deserved—a day we continue to celebrate as Palm Sunday.

The Essential Story

When the disciples got up in the morning, they were expecting another normal day. Now, walking through crowds that lined the street as far as they could see, they were trying to absorb what was going on.

Jesus had sent a couple of them to obtain a donkey and then ridden the animal toward Jerusalem. As he got closer to the big city, word spread that he was coming, and the people responded with great fervor. They spread their cloaks before him on the road, along with palm branches they cut from trees, and their shouts rang out:

> "Hosanna to the Son of David!"
> "Blessed is he who comes in the name of the Lord!"
> "Hosanna in the highest heaven!"
> "Peace in heaven and glory in the highest!"
>
> Matthew 21:9; Luke 19:38

Yet not all the comments were positive. Some Pharisees scolded Jesus and told him to rebuke the crowds praising him. But Jesus was no longer hiding the fact that he was Israel's Messiah. He replied, "I tell you . . . if they keep quiet, the stones will cry out" (Luke 19:40).

Although this was a festive occasion, Jesus wept as he approached Jerusalem. He foresaw not only his rejection by the people but also the coming destruction of the city and temple (which would begin in AD 70). When he arrived in the city, he cleansed the temple by running out its money changers—a "den of robbers" (Luke 19:46)—and he taught there daily until he could no longer do so. Despite the welcome he was receiving, within the week he would be crucified.

Essential Truth

Jesus is too rarely acknowledged for being the King he is, yet we know he delights in praise from those with the spiritual insight to understand his royal position and respond accordingly.

Jesus' Last Supper

Matthew 26:1–29; John 13–17

The Story Continues . . .

The rancor the Jewish leaders felt toward Jesus had been building in intensity for three years, but Jesus' recent resurrection of Lazarus and crowd-pleasing ride into Jerusalem had convinced them in no uncertain terms that something must be done—soon. They didn't really want to kill Jesus during the Feast of the Passover, for fear of the people's response. But when one of Jesus' own apostles offered to betray Jesus, it was the opportunity they'd been looking for.

The Essential Story

It was the strangest Passover dinner Peter had ever attended. Jerusalem was packed as usual, and the disciples had been concerned about where they could have their meal. But Jesus had instructed them to tell a stranger they were coming, and that stranger provided a room for them. It was supposed to be a celebratory meal, a commemoration of Israel's deliverance from Egypt, but Jesus was somber.

They ate for a while, and then Jesus got up, poured water into a bowl, and began to wash the disciples' feet. Peter strongly resisted, but when Jesus firmly stated, "Unless I wash you, you have no part with me" (John 13:8), Peter was all in. Afterward, Jesus told them he had just set an example of service they should emulate.

When Jesus returned to the table, he startled them by saying one of them would soon betray him. Peter motioned to John across the table to ask Jesus who he was talking about. Jesus told John, "It is the one to whom I will give this piece of bread when I have dipped it in the dish" (v. 26). Then he handed the bread to Judas.

Some of the disciples had suspected Judas of embezzling from the group moneybag, and only recently Judas had publicly challenged Jesus after Mary anointed Jesus' feet with expensive perfume (John 12:1–8). Judas expressed indignation that the ointment, which would have cost a year's wages, had not been sold to help the poor. Other disciples had agreed with him, but Jesus understood and defended Mary's action. Only later would the disciples discover that Judas had agreed to betray Jesus to the Pharisees for thirty pieces of silver, and that's why he left the supper that evening.

As Jesus broke the unleavened bread and passed it around, he referred to it as his body. When he passed the wine, he said it was "my blood of the covenant, which is poured out for many for the forgiveness of sins" (Matthew 26:28). Yes, this was a most unusual Passover meal.

Jesus kept talking about leaving, so Peter asked where he was going. Jesus only said, "Where I am going, you cannot follow now, but you will follow later" (John 13:36).

Peter, wanting to encourage Jesus, boldly stated that he would lay down his life for him. In response, Jesus said that by the time the rooster crowed the next morning, Peter would have disowned him three times, but Peter was sure that would never happen.

Jesus then spoke at length about his relationship to God, the disciples' relationship to him, the anticipation of the arrival of the Holy Spirit, the importance of love, the difficulties the disciples should expect, and more. Then he concluded with a prayer of protection for the disciples. There seemed to be a fervency to Jesus' words.

When Jesus finished, they all sang a hymn and headed toward the Mount of Olives, to a quiet garden called Gethsemane.

Essential Truth

Jesus' last supper was a Passover meal that recalled God's great deliverance in the Exodus. Jesus instituted the last supper as an ongoing sacrament by which his disciples, still today, remember his atoning death and their deliverance from sin.

Jesus' Arrest and Trials

Matthew 26:31–27:26; John 18:1–19:16

The Story Continues . . .

Jesus had done his best to prepare his disciples for life after he was gone. He knew they didn't yet comprehend what he was telling them, but it would all make sense after he had completed what he came to do. First, however, it was time for him to undergo the humiliation and pain of a sham trial and undeserved execution.

The Essential Story

Peter and the disciples, except for Judas Iscariot, walked with Jesus to the olive grove known as Gethsemane. Peter had been concerned about Jesus' demeanor at the Passover dinner, and if anything, it had grown worse. Jesus pulled him aside, along with James and John, and told them, "My soul is overwhelmed with sorrow to the point of death. Stay here and keep watch with me" (Matthew 26:38). Then he went a little farther to be alone.

They tried, they really did. But when Jesus returned a short time later, the three of them had fallen asleep. Twice more Jesus left and came back to find them sleeping. One time he was covered with thick sweat from the intensity and anguish of his prayers. No sooner had Jesus returned the third time than the sound of voices and clanging weapons captured their attention. It was Judas, leading a large crowd carrying swords and clubs. Judas kissed Jesus, which was apparently a signal, because several men then stepped forward and seized Jesus.

Peter was carrying a sword, and he instinctively fought back. He swung his weapon but only managed to sever the ear of Malchus, a servant. Jesus told Peter to sheathe his sword. Then he restored Malchus's ear and castigated the mob for sneaking around at night to arrest him even though he had been teaching in the temple every day. While all the attention was on Jesus, the disciples fled.

Peter and John, however, later made their way into the courtyard of the high priest, where they could follow the action of a series of six trials Jesus underwent in quick succession. Three were before his Jewish accusers and three in the Roman courts, where the

Jewish leaders were seeking authority to execute him. The Jewish leaders convicted him on the testimony of false witnesses, and the Roman soldiers beat and bullied him, dressing him in a purple robe and crown of thorns for their own amusement.

Pilate, the governor, was reluctant to convict Jesus. In numerous discussions, he did not perceive Jesus to be a political threat, and he detected that the jealousy of the Jewish leaders was behind most of their hostility. In addition, Pilate's wife had had a troubling dream and urged him, "Don't have anything to do with that innocent man" (Matthew 27:19). He tried to appease Jesus' accusers by having him flogged—a horrendous punishment in itself—but that didn't work. He paired Jesus with a convicted murderer and robber named Barabbas, and he promised to release one of them, yet the contentious crowd chose to kill Jesus. Only after they began to loudly question his loyalty to Caesar did Pilate yield to their request, but not before first publicly washing his hands of the whole affair.

Meanwhile, Judas was agonizing over what he had done. His original motives were unclear. (Some people suggest he was trying to protect Jesus.) But when he saw that Jesus had been condemned, he tried to cancel his deal with the chief priests. They refused to listen, so Judas threw the money on the floor of the temple and went out and hanged himself.

The night wasn't going much better for Peter. He was trying to lie low in the courtyard, but then he was recognized because of his Galilean accent and his association with Jesus. Three separate times he was asked directly if he was one of Jesus' disciples, and all three times he denied it, each time more vehemently. His third denial was punctuated with curses and oaths, and no sooner were the words out of his mouth than he heard a rooster crow. At that moment Jesus made eye contact with him, and all Peter could do was go outside and weep bitterly (Luke 22:60–62). Many more tears would be shed for Jesus over the next three days.

Essential Truth

Jesus was committed to his Father's plan for him to suffer and die, yet he could have opted out at any time (Matthew 26:52–54). His love for humankind caused him to go willingly to the cross and sacrifice himself for our sins.

Jesus' Crucifixion

Matthew 27:27–66

The Story Continues . . .

After Pilate had finally been coerced into authorizing Jesus' death, it was only a short time before Jesus was marched to his crucifixion, bearing his own cross until, physically, he could no longer do so. Crucifixion was savage and inhumane, designed to extend the pain and suffering of death and used only on the worst criminals. Yet while undergoing the most horrific death people could contrive, Jesus continued to model love and compassion for others— even for those who were killing him.

The Essential Story

His time had finally come. Jesus had hoped to somehow avoid this experience, but he was committed to his Father's will. It had been an odd experience to be bound by time. Thirty-three years had quickly dwindled to months, then weeks, then days. Now his mission would be complete in only hours.

Worse than the time boundaries, however, were the limitations of this physical body. Crucifixion was painful beyond description. He was already weakened from the flogging and other abuses of his trial. He'd even needed help carrying his cross to this awful place, this "place of the skull" (Matthew 27:33).

The soldiers had offered him a narcotic, which he declined, although he later asked for a drink. He was trying to stay focused during these final moments of life. He had already forgiven a repentant thief hanging beside him, and he had arranged for John to take care of his mother from now on.

He could see and hear much from the cross. Soldiers were gambling to see who got his clothes, and several women who had faithfully supported his ministry were watching from a distance.

Some people were questioning why he didn't save himself if he was really the Son of God. He didn't bother trying to explain that coming off the cross would prevent their salvation, a gift only the Son of God could provide. Others were sneering and sadistically enjoying his pain and humiliation. He witnessed again how behavior could get ugly when people allowed sin to reign in their lives. He prayed for his Father to forgive them all, because they just couldn't understand.

He also experienced an empty sensation—the universal feeling of abandonment by God when suffering and pain become intense, and he said so by quoting from Psalm 22: "My God, my God, why have you forsaken me?" (v. 1). In his case, though, it was literal abandonment. He was bearing the sins of people past, present, and future—the only time he would ever experience how sin insidiously distances someone from a loving heavenly Father.

Although it was midday, the sky became intensely dark for three hours. Having completed all he came to do, Jesus declared, "It is finished" (John 19:30). He then committed his spirit to God and died. At his death, an earthquake struck with enough power to split rocks and open tombs, after which some long-dead people were seen wandering in the city. The curtain in the temple that hid the holy things of God was torn from top to bottom, an indication that God would be much more approachable from now on, thanks to Jesus.

The sign above the lifeless body of Christ read, in three languages, "Jesus of Nazareth, the King of the Jews" (John 19:19). It was Pilate's final rebuff of the Jewish leaders who had manipulated the system to get what they wanted. Below the cross stood a Roman centurion, among others who had witnessed Jesus' final hours. That short time had been long enough to make an impression on him, because he proclaimed, "Surely he was the Son of God!" (Matthew 27:54).

Some people, even among the Gentiles, were beginning to comprehend the significance of this event. Soon others would follow when they discovered that this was not the end of Jesus' earthly ministry but only a beginning.

Essential Truth

Jesus came into the world to die for the sin of humanity, but as he did he also showed us how to live.

Jesus' Resurrection

Matthew 27:62–28:15; John 19:31–20:31

The Story Continues . . .

Jesus died at midday on a Friday. Sunset that day would have initiated the Sabbath, when such tasks as dealing with the dead were avoided, if not prohibited. Jesus' disciples were frightened and scattered. The faithful women who supported him lacked the influence to take possession of the body. Yet Jesus' body was properly prepared for burial, placed in a sealed tomb, and protected by a Roman guard, making the event of his resurrection all the more spectacular.

The Essential Story

Because the Jewish Sabbath was coming, Roman soldiers were tasked with breaking the legs of the three they had crucified. This took all the sport out of a method of execution designed to maximize and extend pain and suffering, because once the legs were broken, the victims could no longer lift themselves to breathe, forcing suffocation and hastening their deaths. When the soldiers saw Jesus had already died and breaking his legs was unnecessary, one of them plunged a spear into his side instead, releasing a flow of blood and water. Jesus was dead; there could be no doubt.

A short time later, Pilate granted Joseph of Arimathea's special request to take Jesus' body. Joseph, working with Nicodemus (both Pharisees), not only took his body but prepared it for burial. They would have washed the body, applied the seventy-five pounds of spices Nicodemus had brought, and wrapped it with strips of cloth. They placed the body in Joseph's own new tomb and rolled a heavy stone across the entrance.

The Jewish religious leaders knew Jesus was dead, but they anticipated foul play. They knew Jesus had said he would rise after three days, so they asked Pilate for security at the tomb to prevent the disciples from stealing the body (as if Jesus' disciples were in any shape to attempt such a bold move). Pilate ordered the tomb sealed and provided Roman soldiers to guard it.

Yet despite all their efforts, early Sunday morning brought surprises to everyone. Several of the women connected to Jesus' ministry had watched Joseph and Nicodemus bury Jesus, and they returned very early in the morning with spices of their own, perhaps to ensure that the two Pharisees had done an adequate job. But when the women arrived at the tomb, they were greeted by angels who announced Jesus' resurrection and sent them back to tell the apostles the good news. Upon hearing their report, Peter and John rushed to the tomb to see for themselves, and they found the grave clothes neatly folded.

At one point in the confusion of the day, Mary Magdalene was grieving by herself when a man asked her why she was crying. She thought he was the gardener and pleaded for him to show her where Jesus' body was. When the man spoke her name, she realized he was Jesus himself. Jesus would make several other post-resurrection appearances, once to more than five hundred people at the same time (1 Corinthians 15:3–8).

Still, the Jewish leaders tried to explain the disappearance of Jesus' body by paying off the Roman guards who had fled the tomb in terror after the heaven-sent earthquake and an angelic appearance. They promised to protect the soldiers from prosecution (since they could have been put to death for leaving their post) and told them to spread the word that Jesus' disciples had stolen his body. They stuck with that story for a long time, and it still comes up in religious debates today.

What, though, takes more faith? To believe a distressed group of apprehensive and dismayed followers somehow outmaneuvered a trained Roman security force, removed a body from a sealed tomb, and eventually were martyred or otherwise persecuted for their faith without ever revealing the truth? Or to believe Jesus did indeed rise from the dead, just as he repeatedly said he would?

Essential Truth

Jesus' incarnation, sacrificial death, and resurrection are the elements that form the basis of the Christian faith.

Jesus Appears on the Road to Emmaus

Luke 24:13–35

The Story Continues . . .

In the forty days between Jesus' resurrection and his ascension into heaven, he made several random appearances in various locations. More than once he contacted his circle of now eleven disciples. But perhaps no appearance was as unexpected as was his stroll with two otherwise unknown disciples on the road to Emmaus.

The Essential Story

Cleopas and his friend were walking home, trying to make sense of the week's events. They had journeyed to Jerusalem for Passover, and they had probably hoped to see and hear Jesus while there. Now they were reeling from the news of his death and trying to console each other. News was already spreading that the grave had been empty that morning. Was it too much to hope that . . .

A stranger joined them on the road, wanting to know why they looked so sad. They were amazed that he had not heard the news or the rumors beginning to circulate, so they told him what little they knew: Jesus of Nazareth had been a powerful prophet. Many people had hoped he would be the one to redeem Israel, but the chief priests had had him crucified. Yet just that morning his disciples had discovered his tomb was empty. Angels, they said, had told them Jesus was alive!

The stranger gently scolded them for their confusion. He recalled Scripture, going back to Mosaic law and then the writings of the prophets, to review how the Messiah would have to undergo various sufferings before entering his glory. The way this stranger explained it made so much sense!

All too soon they arrived at their village. The stranger started to continue on his way, but when they implored him to stay with them overnight, he agreed. They prepared a meal, and the stranger picked up the bread, thanked God for it, broke it, and handed it to them. At that moment "their eyes were opened" (Luke 24:31). They recognized their visitor was Jesus himself, but as soon as they did, he disappeared.

They were stunned and asked each other, "Were not our hearts burning within us while he talked with us on the road and opened the Scriptures to us?" (v. 32). Although they had just walked the seven miles from Jerusalem to Emmaus, they got up at once and returned to find Jesus' eleven disciples and let them know what had just taken place.

Even while the two were relating their story, Jesus appeared to the group. Still skittish at the end of a long and adrenaline-fueled day, many thought they were seeing a ghost. Jesus calmed them, showed them his scarred hands and feet for verification, and invited them to touch him to ensure they knew he was indeed real. He also asked for some food, and he ate a piece of fish in their presence. Clearly, he wasn't a ghost.

Jesus then "opened their minds" to better understand the significance of all the Scriptures that related to him (v. 45). He promised to do more for them soon, and he told them to wait in Jerusalem until they received, he said, "what my Father has promised" (v. 49).

It would be a fifty-day wait, yet with the knowledge that Jesus was still alive and active, it was a time filled with joy and praise. They could hardly wait to see what else was in store for them.

Essential Truth

Jesus physically rose after death and was seen by many people, verifying his resurrection—the fundamental truth of our Christian faith.

Peter Renews His Commitment to Jesus

John 21

The Story Continues . . .

Many of Jesus' post-resurrection appearances appeared to be somewhat brief and for the purpose of confirming that he was indeed alive. In one case, however, he spent an extended time with several of his closest disciples to assure them of his love, forgive their previous lapses in faith, and get them back on track.

The Essential Story

"I'm going out to fish" (John 21:3). Peter didn't know how to fill all the time on his hands now that Jesus was no longer there to lead them, but he knew how to fish, as did many of the others. Six more disciples went with him.

Professional fishermen usually worked at night, so the catch would be fresh for the markets in the morning, but the group had a disappointing night and hadn't caught anything. Early in the morning a figure on shore called out to ask how they were doing, and they shared their frustration with him. He told them, "Throw your net on the right side of the boat and you will find some" (v. 6).

They had nothing to lose, and when they took his advice, they caught so many fish that they couldn't haul the net into the boat. It must have been eerily reminiscent of a similar miraculous catch of fish the day Jesus first called them to be his disciples (Luke 5:1–11). John realized it at once and told Peter, "It is the Lord!" (John 21:7).

They were only a hundred yards from shore, so Peter hardly took the time to drape himself before leaping into the water and swimming for shore. The others sailed in, pulling the net of fish along behind them. They found a charcoal fire burning, on which were fish and bread. (The last charcoal fire Peter had smelled was probably the one in the high priest's courtyard the night he had denied Jesus three times [John 18:18]). Jesus told them to bring some of the fish they had caught, so Peter dragged the net ashore and inventoried the fish—153 in all. It was a hefty catch, yet the nets, which needed to be repaired with great regularity, had not broken.

After breakfast, Jesus pulled Peter aside and three times asked him, "Do you love me?" (vv. 15–17). Peter affirmed his love for Jesus all three times, though it pained him to hear the repeated question. This was an opportunity for Peter to offset his three previous denials with three affirmations, yet Jesus also wanted to prepare Peter to expect a martyr's death. But rather than asking Jesus any probing follow-up questions on this occasion, Peter wanted to know instead what was going to happen to John. Jesus told him, in so many words, that it was none of his business. Peter's main concern should be to simply follow Jesus from now on.

Peter's return to fishing was a short-lived pursuit. Despite all his denials and missteps along the way, he was ready days later when the Holy Spirit came to empower and enable the believers in Christ to reach out to the rest of the world. Peter was the one who stood up and proclaimed the Gospel to the international crowds in Jerusalem. Jesus' previous words to him came true that day: "I tell you that you are Peter, and on this rock I will build my church, and the gates of Hades will not overcome it" (Matthew 16:18).

Essential Truth

When we make mistakes or come up short on our spiritual journeys (as we all sometimes do), we must not allow those slips to halt our progress. With Jesus' forgiveness and support, we can keep moving forward.

STORIES OF THE EARLY CHURCH

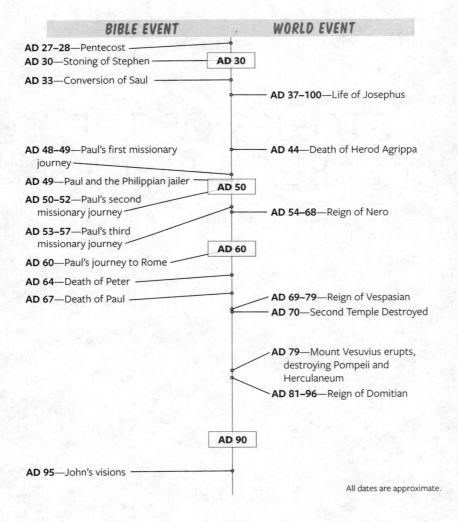

BIBLE EVENT   WORLD EVENT

AD 27–28—Pentecost

AD 30—Stoning of Stephen   AD 30

AD 33—Conversion of Saul

AD 37–100—Life of Josephus

AD 48–49—Paul's first missionary journey

AD 44—Death of Herod Agrippa

AD 49—Paul and the Philippian jailer   AD 50

AD 50–52—Paul's second missionary journey

AD 54–68—Reign of Nero

AD 53–57—Paul's third missionary journey

AD 60

AD 60—Paul's journey to Rome

AD 64—Death of Peter

AD 67—Death of Paul

AD 69–79—Reign of Vespasian

AD 70—Second Temple Destroyed

AD 79—Mount Vesuvius erupts, destroying Pompeii and Herculaneum

AD 81–96—Reign of Domitian

AD 90

AD 95—John's visions

All dates are approximate.

The Holy Spirit Arrives at Pentecost

Acts 2

The Story Continues . . .

Pentecost was celebrated fifty days after Passover. Jesus had been crucified at Passover, and after his resurrection he spent forty days making various appearances to encourage believers before he ascended into heaven. His final instructions were for his followers to stay in Jerusalem and wait for what he said was "the gift my Father promised"—the baptism of the Holy Spirit (Acts 1:1–5). It wouldn't be a long wait.

The Essential Story

One hundred and twenty of Jesus' followers were waiting—exactly for what and for how long, they didn't know. Jesus had made occasional appearances for a few weeks, but for several days now, nothing. Crowds were returning to Jerusalem to celebrate Pentecost, a harvest festival. Meanwhile, the believers passed the time by tending to business as much as possible. One action was to select another apostle to replace Judas Iscariot. Two men were nominated, and they cast lots to determine which one was God's choice. It would be the last time they would need to use that method to determine God's will.

They had found an upper room where they could assemble, and they were all together on the day of Pentecost when the sound of a powerful wind filled the room. A visible manifestation of what looked like tongues of fire descended on each one of them. As they experienced the filling of the Holy Spirit, they found themselves able to speak in the native languages of all the visitors in Jerusalem.

They immediately had everyone's attention. What appeared to be an unschooled group of Galileans whose leader had recently died was suddenly describing the mighty works of God in dozens of other tongues. Some people responded with perplexed amazement; others presumed they were drunk on cheap wine.

Peter took charge, standing and delivering a speech to explain that this event was the fulfillment of a prophecy from their prophet Joel that said one day God would "pour out [his] Spirit," and that "everyone who calls on the name of the Lord will be saved" (Acts 2:17, 21). He told them that Jesus had been sent from God, yet his own people had had him killed. The person they had crucified was "both Lord and Messiah" (v. 36).

Many in the crowd took Peter's words to heart, and they wanted to know what to do. He told them, "Repent and be baptized, every one of you, in the name of Jesus Christ for the forgiveness of your sins. And you will receive the gift of the Holy Spirit" (v. 38). Three thousand people took him up on his offer that day, and the church was born.

It was a thrilling time for those believers who were growing in the power of the Holy Spirit. The apostles were performing miracles much like Jesus had done. A spirit of sharing was strong among them, as those who had wealth and possessions gave them to those who didn't. They were eating together, growing spiritually, and increasing in number every day.

They would experience growing pains soon enough, but for a while, every day was filled with awe and wonder.

Essential Truth

On Pentecost, God's Holy Spirit came to dwell in his followers. This same Holy Spirit still lives in all who choose to be disciples of Jesus, providing everything they need for whatever he has called them to do.

Ananias and Sapphira

Acts 4:32–5:11

The Story Continues . . .

The young church was quickly expanding, and as happens so often with rapid growth, problems arose. For one thing, many of the same religious leaders who had opposed Jesus were just as vigilant in attacking the ever-growing group of believers. Some of the apostles were imprisoned for nothing more than speaking out about what they believed, but their jail sentences only inspired prayers for greater boldness. The more serious problems, they were about to discover, were internal.

The Essential Story

Sapphira and her husband, Ananias, were intrigued by this new religious movement. At last count, the number of believers was up to five thousand men (Acts 4:4), plus surely that many or more women and children. The preaching and miracles being performed were big draws for a lot of people, but the lifestyle modeled by the believers attracted even more. She had never seen such willingness to share without restraint and without being asked. Even with all those members, no one was in need.

One specific believer had gained the apostles' attention. His name was Joseph, but he was so consistent in his generosity and character that the apostles started calling him Barnabas, meaning "son of encouragement" (v. 36). On one occasion he sold a field and brought the money for it right to the apostles, so the name had stuck. Now *everyone* was calling him Barnabas.

Well, Sapphira and Ananias had property too. They got to talking one day and decided they could part with it for the good of the church. As they continued to talk, though, the thought crossed their minds that they didn't necessarily have to give it *all* to the apostles. But then, wouldn't that make them sound more selfish than "Mr. Encouragement"? Yes, it might.

But what if they held back a part for themselves and donated the rest of the money with a statement like "Here's what we got for our property"? That would work. After all, who would be the wiser? They got their story straight, set aside the portion they wanted to keep, and then Ananias went to give the rest to the apostles. When he didn't come home in the next three hours, Sapphira went to check on him.

Peter greeted her, and for some reason all the people with him looked nervous, even fearful. Peter asked her, "Tell me, is this the price you and Ananias got for the land?" (Acts 5:8). She told him it was. Peter stared at her, grimly, and said, "How could you conspire to test the Spirit of the Lord? Listen! The feet of the men who buried your husband are at the door, and they will carry you out also" (v. 9).

Those were the last words she heard before she fell, dead. She didn't get to hear the explanation that Ananias had heard right before *he* died. The two of them had every right to keep part of their wealth for themselves; the ruse they had attempted to pull on the church was the problem. They thought they were pulling a fast one on the apostles, but they had lied to the Holy Spirit. They had lied to God.

The consequences suffered by Ananias and Sapphira were not lost on the church. Great fear fell upon the believers as they realized that the Spirit who was the source of such joy and power in their lives was, in fact, God. As the fledgling church continued to grow, the believers would know that the loving God who was so gracious to them could not be fooled or manipulated.

Essential Truth

In serving a Lord who is "the way and the truth and the life" (John 14:6), many of the offenses people classify as minor sins or little white lies may be more serious than they realize.

Two Miraculous Prison Releases

Acts 5:12–42; 12:1–24

The Story Continues . . .

Jesus had told his followers to expect persecution. Opposition to God would continue after his death, and anyone who spoke for God would be a target. Sometimes God would deliver his people in miraculous ways, but during this period many of them were martyred for their faith. It's believed that most of Jesus' original twelve apostles were eventually put to death for the truth they proclaimed.

The Essential Story

They were only trying to minister to the people as the Spirit led them to do. They were teaching about Jesus, curing the sick, healing the people of various infirmities, and casting out evil spirits. And for that, the jealous Sadducees had thrown the apostles into prison.

They weren't there long, however. That very night an angel appeared, opened the prison doors, led them out, and told them to get back to work. At daybreak they were again teaching in the temple. Meanwhile, the Sanhedrin (a court comprising Jewish religious leaders) had convened to conduct the apostles' trial, and they sent for them. Confused officers returned to report that although the prison doors were locked, and the guards had not left their posts, the apostles were nowhere to be found. Then someone else came in and reported that the apostles were speaking at the temple.

The leaders sent for them and reminded them they had been warned not to talk about Jesus. They replied that they "must obey God rather than human beings!" (Acts 5:29). Some of the Sanhedrin wanted to have them put to death, especially after they accused the Jewish leaders of being responsible for the death of Jesus, but a wise leader named Gamaliel called for reason. Citing previous religious movements that had failed, he said, "Leave these men alone! Let them go! For if their purpose or activity is of human origin, it will fail. But if it is from God, you will not be able to stop these men; you will only find yourselves fighting against God" (vv. 38–39). So instead the court had them beaten and released, and the apostles left rejoicing because they had been found worthy to suffer, much as Jesus had suffered.

Evoking jealousy among the Jewish leaders was one problem; being perceived as a threat to the civil government was quite another. King Herod had arrested several believers, including James, the apostle who was the brother of John. When his approval rating went up after he had James killed, Herod had Peter seized and arrested, intending to kill him as well. The church prayed earnestly for Peter.

The night before Peter's scheduled trial he was guarded by Roman soldiers, sleeping between two of them while bound with two chains, as sentries stood watch. An angel woke him and told him to get dressed. Peter's chains fell off, and the angel led him out of the prison as they passed the guards and saw the gates open for them. Peter thought he was seeing a vision, but then he found himself outside on the street. He made his way to a nearby meeting of believers, but he couldn't get them to open the door at first because of their shock and excitement. They later helped him leave the area to elude Herod.

When Herod discovered that Peter had somehow escaped incarceration, he ordered Peter's guards put to death. But proud Herod soon met his own demise. A delegation went to him, seeking a favor, and he delivered an official and impressive oration. The listeners, wanting to keep him in a good mood, chanted, "This is the voice of a god, not of a man" (Acts 12:22). Herod soaked up their adoration rather than giving praise to God, and he died as a result. The official cause of death? "An angel of the Lord struck him down, and he was eaten by worms and died" (v. 23).

Essential Truth

Disciples aren't always spared suffering or death simply because they're believers, yet they frequently experience God's protection and provision.

The Stoning of Stephen

Acts 6:1–8:3

The Story Continues . . .

As the number of church members rose rapidly, the apostles soon realized they needed more help. They chose seven men to serve as deacons and handle the more practical, mundane aspects of ministry. Yet some of the deacons were soon making names for themselves as God worked through them in powerful ways. One would discover the backlash of such fame in the religiously and politically charged environment of first-century Judea.

The Essential Story

Something had to be done about this new movement that had suddenly arisen after the death of their leader, Jesus. It should have died out by now, but for some reason it seemed to spread more every day. Young Saul was concerned as he watched the trial of Stephen. The fellow had testified that his primary responsibility was to make sure everyone in his group got enough food, yet he had been seen doing much more.

Not only had Stephen been reported to be out working miracles; he was also a skilled debater. Several of the most knowledgeable Jewish leaders had publicly spoken against Stephen, but he had surprising wisdom, and he managed to put them to shame. If he and the other Jesus followers would just keep to themselves and quit their proselytizing, they could go believe whatever they wanted. But they were out in public every day, talking about Jesus. What kind of group revered a crucified leader? Yet even many of the traditional Jewish priests were starting to believe, so *something* had to be done—and soon.

In Stephen's case, the Sanhedrin had arranged for some witnesses to accuse him of false teaching and blasphemy, so they could put him on trial. Even though he knew the charges were contrived, Stephen wasn't rattled. He sat before them confident and peaceful, with the face of an angel. When given the opportunity to defend himself, he launched into a long and detailed history of Israel, as if they didn't know about Abraham, Joseph, Jacob, Moses, Joshua, David, Solomon, and others. Yet Stephen's emphasis was on the repeated disobedience of the Jewish people, and he had the audacity to put the Sanhedrin members in that category.

The more he talked, the angrier his accusers became. But what sealed his fate was his concluding comment: "Look, . . . I see heaven open and the Son of Man standing at the right hand of God" (Acts 7:56). The judges became a furious mob as they covered their ears, yelling as loudly as they could, and they dragged Stephen out of the city. They told Saul to take care of their coats while they stoned Stephen to death. Even then, Stephen was heard praying "Lord Jesus, receive my spirit" and "Lord, do not hold this sin against them" (vv. 59–60).

At least Stephen's execution had sparked a united persecution against the church, driving many of the believers out of Jerusalem into Judea and Samaria. But it was like trying to stamp out a campfire; new groups of Jesus-following communities reignited in many of the places where believers relocated.

As he realized someone needed to go out, round up these rebellious members of The Way (Acts 9:2), and put an end to this movement once and for all, Saul saw a new purpose for his life.

Essential Truth

Stephen was the first martyr, but untold believers throughout the ages have died for their faith, confident that death is neither something to be feared nor an ultimate end to their relationship with God.

The Conversion of Saul (Paul)

Acts 9:1–19; 22:3–21; 26:12–23

The Story Continues . . .

Stephen's stoning had been a catalyst for action against the rapidly growing church, whose teachings about Jesus were contradicting many Jewish beliefs and traditions that had been faithfully followed for many centuries. It was therefore necessary for Jewish leadership to intensify their efforts to put an end to the church. Saul had endorsed Stephen's killing but had played only a minor role in it. He was ready for a much greater commitment.

The Essential Story

There was always paperwork, it seemed, but Saul had it with him. He had petitioned the high priest for official permission to travel to Damascus, seek out any Jesus followers (male or female), and have them bound and returned to Jerusalem for trial. Now he had not only the passion but also the authority to arrest and transport believers in The Way. He was near the end of this 135-mile trip, and he was eager to get to work.

But suddenly he and his companions were hit with a heavenly spotlight, which Paul described later as "brighter than the sun" (Acts 26:13), and they fell to the ground. All of them heard a noise, but only Saul understood that it was a voice speaking to him: "Saul, Saul, why do you persecute me?" (Acts 9:4). He asked who was speaking, and the voice said, "I am Jesus, whom you are persecuting. . . . Now get up and go into the city, and you will be told what you must do" (v. 5).

Saul opened his eyes wide, but he couldn't see. His entourage had to lead him by the hand the rest of the way to Damascus, where he spent three days fasting before a man named Ananias showed up. Saul still couldn't see, but the guy sounded nervous, perhaps even frightened. Apparently, Saul's reputation had preceded him. Ananias somehow knew about Saul's vision of Jesus, and he said he had been sent to restore Saul's sight. Ananias laid his hands on Saul, and then a scaly substance fell from Saul's eyes. Saul could see. He got up, was baptized right away, and got something to eat.

Saul connected with other believers in Damascus who, like Ananias, were probably tentative and skeptical at first. But soon he was preaching in the synagogue, proclaiming with certainty that Jesus was the Son of God. In a matter of days, the Damascus Jews were conspiring to kill Saul. They staked out the city gates, looking for an opportunity, but the disciples put Saul in a basket and lowered him from the city wall, allowing him to escape.

Back in Jerusalem, Saul again had difficulty gaining the confidence of believers. This time it was Barnabas who courageously stepped forward and helped him be accepted by the group. When Saul's bold preaching about Jesus once more attracted others who wanted him dead, the church members helped him escape to Tarsus, his hometown.

As the church continued to grow, Saul would soon take the good news about Jesus to a whole new demographic—the Gentiles. He would adopt a more Greek-sounding name, Paul. And in helping others understand the marvelous power of God, he would come back repeatedly to this compelling story of his conversion on the road to Damascus.

Essential Truth

The love and power of Christ can turn even the most zealous and vehement critic into a dynamic and determined evangelist.

Peter's Vision

Acts 10

The Story Continues . . .

While Saul (later Paul) was coming to grips with what God had planned for him, Peter continued to lead the church. He displayed great power, including healing a paralyzed man who had been unable to move for eight years and even raising a woman from the dead (Acts 9:32–43). But primarily, he proclaimed Christ. After Philip's ministry in Samaria had been surprisingly productive, Peter and John went there and saw many Samaritans profess belief and receive the Holy Spirit (Acts 8:4–25). That was a surprise, considering the long-standing rift between Jews and Samaritans. But even bigger surprises were coming.

The Essential Story

Roman centurions weren't easily frightened, but Cornelius was terrified. In Caesarea, where gods were many and religion often bordered on superstition, Cornelius had come to believe in the true

God. He prayed regularly, gave to those in need, and tried to live and raise his family right. Other than that, Gentiles didn't have much of a way to connect with the God of the Jews.

But an angel had just appeared to Cornelius in a vision, suddenly and unexpectedly, and called him by name. Shakily he asked, "What is it, Lord?" (Acts 10:4). The angel affirmed Cornelius's faithfulness and desire to serve God, and then the angel told him to send for a man in Joppa named Peter, who was staying with a tanner named Simon. Cornelius dispatched three men right away for the thirty-mile trip to Joppa.

Meanwhile, in Joppa the next day, Peter was hungry. He went to the rooftop to pray while his lunch was being prepared. He fell into a trance and saw a large sheet descend from heaven, containing all kinds of animals, reptiles, and birds. A voice told him to "Get up, Peter. Kill and eat" (v. 13).

Peter was repulsed at the thought. Many of those food sources were unclean—clearly forbidden by Mosaic law. Yet the voice was insistent: "Do not call anything impure that God has made clean" (v. 15). This happened three times before the sheet was taken away. Peter was still confused, trying to figure out what his vision meant, when Cornelius's messengers arrived at the door. The Holy Spirit let Peter know in advance that the arrival of the three visitors was not coincidental and that he should return with them. They explained why they had come, and Peter went with them the next day, taking with him some other believers from Joppa.

Cornelius had also assembled several friends and family members in Caesarea. When Peter arrived, Cornelius recounted his vision, and Peter shared what God was trying to teach him about redefining what was or wasn't unclean. As Peter taught about Jesus, the Holy Spirit fell on everyone present, including the Gentiles, who started speaking in tongues and praising God. The Jewish believers with Peter were astonished at this occurrence (v. 45). Peter had the new believers baptized, and he stayed with them a few days.

Somewhat reluctantly at first, the church began to include Gentiles based only on their faith, without the necessity of circumcision, dietary requirements, or other traditional requirements. Their full acceptance would not be without controversy and turmoil. But thanks to Cornelius, they were off to a good start.

Essential Truth

Jesus' sacrificial death was to atone for the sins of the entire world and not for just one particular sect. All are now invited to find forgiveness and salvation in Jesus.

Paul and the Philippian Jailer

Acts 16:6–40

The Story Continues . . .

After Paul's conversion, he quickly became a dynamo of Christian evangelism. He took the Gospel to new territories and started churches to strengthen believers after he moved on. He spoke with confidence and authority, and he performed numerous healing miracles in Jesus' name. To his alarm, in one city he was worshiped as a god. In another he brought a young man back from the dead. But frequently he faced strong opposition and underwent tremendous trials (2 Corinthians 11:23–28). Still, positive results frequently came from his sufferings, as in his experience in Philippi.

The Essential Story

"These men are servants of the Most High God, who are telling you the way to be saved" (Acts 16:17). The slave girl had been following them, repeating the same message for days now. It's not that the spirit possessing her wasn't speaking the truth, but the continual repetition had grown from a distraction to an outright annoyance.

Paul and Silas had been in Philippi for only a few days, directed to their first European location by God through a vision. But upon arrival they couldn't even find a synagogue in this Roman colony. The first audience they found was a group of women by the riverside, at least one of whom was already a believer in God. As Paul told them about Jesus, this woman, Lydia, responded to Paul's message and was baptized. She was well-to-do, and she invited Paul and his companions to stay at her house.

Yet no sooner had Paul begun to minister in Philippi than this possessed girl started trailing behind him, repeating, "These men are servants . . ." He'd had enough, and he finally commanded the spirit to leave. The girl was instantly freed, but she lost the ability to tell the future, which meant a loss of income for her owners. A conflict ensued, and Paul and Silas didn't have the hometown advantage. They were immediately dragged to the city magistrates and, without benefit of a trial, were stripped, beaten, and then imprisoned. The jailer, ordered to secure them carefully, put them in stocks in an inner cell of the prison.

Paul and Silas had a most unusual response to being beaten and incarcerated. At midnight they were praying and singing hymns as the other prisoners listened in. A sudden earthquake shook the prison—a peculiar earthquake that released all the prisoners' bonds and opened all the prison doors. The sleeping jailer woke with alarm, anticipating Rome's punishment for allowing the escape of those under his watch, and he prepared to take his own life. But Paul quickly assured him that all were accounted for and urged him not to harm himself.

The jailer wasn't sure what was going on, but he realized the earthquake was somehow connected to Paul and Silas. Trembling, he asked them, "What must I do to be saved?" (v. 30). Paul told him about the love and sacrifice of Jesus, and the jailer was immediately baptized along with his family. In addition, he washed the men's wounds and fed them—not out of obligation or to repay a favor but because he felt joy unlike any he'd ever known.

The next morning word came from the magistrates to release Paul and Silas, but Paul wasn't satisfied to leave quietly. They had been publicly accused, and he wanted a public acquittal. When he told them he and Silas were Roman citizens, the breach of their legal rights alarmed the city officials. They personally escorted the two from the prison, but they also asked them to please leave the city.

They moved on to the next town and the next challenge to their faith, but not before a final visit of encouragement to Lydia and the other group of new believers. It seemed that worshipers in Philippi were going to be primarily Gentiles and women. The church of Jesus Christ was becoming a religious organization unlike anything its Jewish founders—or anyone else, for that matter—had ever seen.

Essential Truth

Productive ministry frequently results for those who learn to deal graciously with unplanned circumstances and with people unlike themselves.

Paul's Journey to Rome

Acts 27:1–28:16

The Story Continues . . .

Paul had completed three lengthy missionary journeys and experienced all kinds of triumphs and tribulations. But back in

Jerusalem another conflict with Jewish religious leaders led to an arrest (primarily for his protective custody), followed by an ongoing imprisonment. At one point he sat in jail for two years while the Roman procurator hoped to receive a bribe from him (Acts 24:24–27). A short time later Paul, using his rights as a Roman citizen, appealed to have his case tried by Caesar, which necessitated a trip to Rome. The journey, however, did not go as expected.

The Essential Story

Paul had tried to warn them that it was too late in the season for the sea voyage they had planned, but he was a tentmaker and an evangelist—and a prisoner—so the Roman centurion had listened to the ship's pilot instead. After changing vessels once already, they were still headed for Rome, where he was to stand trial. He was on a grain ship out of Egypt carrying the crew, other prisoners, and some passengers—276 people in all. God had previously assured Paul he would get there safely (Acts 23:11), but the crew seemed less certain of safe arrival with each passing day.

The ship was passing Crete when a northeaster blew in with hurricane-force winds. At the mercy of the storm, the crew did all they could over a three-day period to stay afloat: pull in the lifeboat that was filling with water, tie the ship together to the best of their ability, and throw any unnecessary cargo or equipment overboard. Still, they went days without seeing either daylight or stars, and despair was setting in.

During all the commotion one night, an angel appeared to Paul. The next day Paul assured everyone that indeed the ship would run aground and be destroyed, but the people would all survive. After a couple of weeks on the Adriatic Sea, the crew sensed they were approaching land, so they dropped anchor and prayed for morning to come. Some of the experienced sailors tried to slip away in the lifeboat, but Paul warned the centurion that he would not guarantee their safety unless everyone stayed together. The centurion ordered soldiers to cut the ropes and let the boat go.

Many hadn't eaten in a long while, and Paul encouraged them to do so and gain their strength. In the morning, when they could see, they cut loose the anchors and made for a sandy beach, but the boat hit a reef and began to break apart. The soldiers planned to kill the prisoners to prevent their escape, but the centurion forbade it for Paul's sake. And just as Paul had assured them, they all made it safely to shore.

They were on Malta, and the inhabitants were friendly and helpful. It was a cold and rainy day, so they built a fire to warm the survivors. Paul was adding wood to the fire when a poisonous snake struck him and attached to his hand. He held it over the fire until it let go, and the people watched and waited, believing he must be guilty of something terrible to survive a shipwreck only to die of snakebite. But when nothing happened, they presumed he must be a god.

An island official who lived nearby invited a group to his home. His father was suffering from fever and dysentery. Paul prayed and healed the man, prompting other diseased islanders to come out and be cured. In response, they provided new supplies for the group still headed for Rome.

Paul did arrive safely, as he was promised. He would spend another two years awaiting trial, but during that time he had relative freedom and wrote several of his epistles. A church historian later wrote that Paul was eventually released and continued his ministry until he was again arrested and, at that time, martyred. But in one of his final letters, Paul proclaimed with confidence, "I have fought the good fight, I have finished the race, I have kept the faith. Now there is in store for me the crown of righteousness, which the Lord, the righteous Judge, will award to me on that day" (2 Timothy 4:7–8).

Essential Truth

Paul both taught and modeled how, even during unpleasant events, peace and joy are possible for those who remain faithful—and focused on—Jesus.

John's Visions

Revelation 1; 21–22

The Story Continues . . .

While many of the first believers in Jesus were martyred for their faith (including, according to church tradition, Paul and most of the original apostles), the apostle John lived to be an old man. He did not escape his own tribulations, however. He was exiled to a small island in the Aegean Sea "because of the word of God and the testimony of Jesus" (Revelation 1:9). Yet this attempt to stop him from spreading the word about his Lord only increased its reach exponentially. On the island of Patmos, John had incredible visions of Jesus and of events to come. John's apocalyptic writings became Scripture, and his written testimony continues to be discussed and debated to this day.

The Essential Story

He had been instructed to "write on a scroll what you see" (Revelation 1:11), and John had been doing that. He was just glad he didn't have to explain everything he was seeing.

Among his many bizarre and confusing visions, the first one was perfectly clear. The source of his visions was Jesus, who appeared while John was in the Spirit. But this was not the unassuming rabbi John had followed for three years. This materialization of his Lord was Jesus in all his glory—radiating brilliance like the sun, with eyes like blazing fire and a voice like the roar of an ocean. John had fallen at his feet, as if dead. And lest there be any doubt as to the figure's identity, he spoke: "Do not be afraid. I am the First and the Last. I am the Living One; I was dead, and now look, I am alive for ever and ever! And I hold the keys of death and Hades. Write, therefore, what you have seen, what is now and what will take place" (vv. 17–19).

John had written and written. The eyewitness account of his visions was to go out to seven churches in Asia, with a personal message attached to each one (Revelation 2–3). He had been shown amazing sights: God's throne in heaven; a sealed scroll that could be opened only by "a Lamb, looking as if it had been slain" (Revelation 5:6); four horsemen bringing war, famine, and death; mighty angels with trumpets announcing plague after plague upon the earth; a threatening dragon; a powerful beast and a great prostitute; a climactic battle at a place called Armageddon; a mysterious number 666; and much more. Through all these visions he saw unprecedented persecution of anyone who remained faithful to Christ, including bloodshed and martyrdom for multitudes.

But just when it looked as if evil would win out, John saw heaven opened and the arrival of a warrior Christ on a white horse, leading the armies of heaven. Their victory was instantaneous. Satan was bound, the beast (Antichrist) was thrown into a fiery lake of burning sulfur, and their followers were judged and put to death.

After all the horrific scenes John had witnessed, his final vision was a glorious one. He saw "the Holy City, the new Jerusalem" descending from heaven, announced as "God's dwelling place . . . now among the people" (Revelation 21:2–3). John was invited to take a closer look. The foursquare city had streets of gold, surrounded by a jasper wall built on foundations comprising all sorts of precious stones. Each gate was made of a single pearl. The gates were inscribed with the names of the twelve tribes of Israel, and the foundations were inscribed with the names of the twelve apostles. But none of that was the most impressive part.

What was most memorable was that the perpetual brilliance of the city came from God on his throne. The illumination and constant access to God's presence had eliminated any need for sun, moon, or temple. A crystal river flowing with the water of life came from the throne, and beside it was the Tree of Life bearing fruit year-round. The city was a place with no more death, crying, pain, or darkness. God himself would wipe away any tear.

After all the mystery and metaphor associated with John's apocalyptic writings, he ended with a clear and unmistakable message: Jesus is coming soon, after putting an end to sin and evil, and all who are willing are invited to come to him.

Essential Truth

Scripture concludes as it began. Although it was destroyed by sin in Eden, the original intimate relationship between God and humanity will one day be restored for eternity.

Acknowledgments

Thank you to the outstanding team at Bethany House for catching the vision for this book. Thanks especially to Andy McGuire and Jean Kavich Bloom for your editorial support—your insights made this a better book! We appreciate the others who contributed to the book as well: Rob Williams, Brian Brunsting, Jolene Steffer, and Jeanne Hedrick. And thanks to the Steve Laube Agency for your help to turn this dream into a reality.

About the Authors

Christopher D. Hudson is the author of the *Self-Guided Tour of the Bible*, *Navigating the Bible*, *Once-A-Day at the Table Family Devotional*, *Following Jesus Daily Devotional*, and *100 Names of God Daily Devotional*, and has contributed to over fifty Bible projects. He has consulted with the Museum of the Bible, and he oversaw the development and launch of their initial books into the marketplace. Christopher is a graduate of Wheaton College and has been an active teacher in his church for over twenty years. He lives outside Chicago with his wife and three children.

Stan Campbell holds communication degrees from Middle Tennessee State University and Wheaton College. He is a career writer and editor with over twenty years of youth ministry experience. He has authored dozens of Bible-related books, primarily for youth and seeker markets, including the first three editions of *The Complete Idiot's Guide to the Bible*. He and his wife, Kathy, live in the Nashville area.